CHURCHES AND TURTON

David J Leeming

Publication No 31 September 2008

No 31 Churches and Chapels of Turton
David J Leeming
Published by Turton Local History Society September 2008
ISBN 978-1-904974-31-4

This book is dedicated to my friend and colleague the late Richard Seddon.

TURTON LOCAL HISTORY SOCIETY

Turton Local History Society exists to promote an interest in history by discussion, research and record. It is particularly concerned with the history of the former Urban District of Turton and its constituent ancient townships of Bradshaw, Edgworth, Entwistle, Harwood, Longworth, Quarlton and Turton. Meetings are held from September to May inclusive, at 7.30pm on the third Tuesday of the month at the Barlow Institute, Edgworth. Visitors are welcome.

Previous publications are listed on the inside front cover. In recognition of the years of research undertaken and as a matter of courtesy and good academic practice, it is expected that due acknowledgement will be made to the author and Turton Local History Society when any further use is made of the contents of this publication.

PREFACE

In this book are described the various churches and chapels that exist, or have existed, in the parishes of Turton and Walmsley. The national and local events are covered that led to the evolution of Christian places of worship up to recent times. To keep the book to a manageable size and avoid repetition of published work, the townships of Harwood and Bradshaw have been excluded although they would normally form part of our area of interests. Several of the older buildings described herein have now been demolished or converted to other uses. Many of them were landmarks in the local area, had character, and with few exceptions were of high quality, built of stone or brick, originally and specifically for Christian worship. If walls could have spoken over the years, these fine places would have been well able to tell their own stories in far more detail than the chapters chronicled in this publication. In past times, each church and chapel in a particular neighbourhood, irrespective of its denomination, functioned to a large extent autonomously, both religiously and socially, although rarely in complete isolation from its neighbouring church, chapel or community.

CONTENTS Page

ILLUSTRATIONS

CHAPTER 1 CHRISTIANITY IN ENGLAND

1.1 Early Christianity in England

Following the birth of Christ, Christianity entered England in the wake of the Romans who colonised the country in AD 43. Initially Christianity was illegal but eventually, in AD 325, became the official religion in the Roman Empire and must have been widespread at that time. There is a Roman Road (Watling Street) in our area and no doubt that it was once part of Roman Britain. However, after the withdrawal of the legions, and invasion by pagan Anglo-Saxons, Christianity disappeared leaving no surviving structure or artefacts in this part of the country.

Christianity survived in Ireland and by the 4th century it was being carried into some coastal areas, including Cornwall, Wales and Northumberland, by monks of the Celtic Church. Eventually in AD 597 Pope Gregory sent St Augustine to convert the Anglo-Saxon tribes of England to the Christianity of Rome.

St. Augustine converted Ethelbert King of Kent and became archbishop in AD 601. His original intent was to establish an archbishopric in London, but London was then in the realm of decidedly pagan tribes, so Canterbury, the capital of the Kentish kingdom, became the seat of the pre-eminent archbishop of England. Augustine also introduced St. Benedict's vision of a monastic system that was to last in England until the Reformation. A wide variety of monastic orders ensued including Benedictines, Cistercians, Augustinians, Carthusians, etc.

In 603 St Augustine tried to unite the Roman and Celtic churches but there was too much conflict with the pagan religions and between the two churches. Even Easter was celebrated on different days by the two traditions. The Celtic Church was ascetic, fervent, based on monastic life, and loosely organised whereas the Roman Church was more structured and disciplined. Finally the two Christian traditions united under the Roman Church after the Synod of Whitby in AD 664.

Before the Norman Conquest England was divided into separate Anglo-Saxon kingdoms: Northumbria, Mercia, York, Lindsey, East Anglia, Kent, and Wessex. The various kingdoms then vied for supremacy until AD 829 when they accepted Egbert of Wessex as overlord and, in AD 946, became unified under Eadred. Also, there were lengthy periods between the 9th and 11th centuries when the Danish kings, based in York, ruled large parts of England. Cathedrals were established more or less in a central position in each Anglo-Saxon Kingdom. In Mercia a cathedral was established at Lichfield, which became important for our area. York was second only to Canterbury and became the main cathedral in the northern province of England.

Throughout the Dark Ages and the mediaeval period the monasteries were almost the only repository of scholarship. The monks and nuns were often the only educated members of society. They were most numerous during the early 14th century when there were as many as 500 different houses. The Black Death of AD 1348 dealt them a hard blow from which many never fully recovered.

1.2 Early local Christianity

The church at Bolton was initially in the Province of York but in late Anglo-Saxon times moved into the See of Mercia in the Province of Canterbury. Between AD 650 and 1541 the seat of the Bishop of Mercia moved several times. In 656 it was at Lichfield, in 1079 at Chester, in 1095 at Coventry and a few years later at Lichfield again, where it remained until 1541.

When the parish of Bolton-le-Moors was first established, the district was very sparsely inhabited and the boundaries had to be extended widely over the surrounding countryside to make the church worthwhile and generate enough income to support the necessary clergy. The upshot was to create, in Bolton-le-Moors, one of the largest parishes in the country, which in due course had to be divided into townships, to facilitate local government functions traditionally provided by the parish in other parts of the country. As church attendance was then compulsory, several remote subsidiary chapels called ‘chapels of ease’ gradually came into use to spare people in outlying districts from the long walk to the parish church.

A parish church in Bolton was built about AD 1100 by a Norman lord on the site of a Saxon structure, as some curiously carved sculptures and a stone cross testify. The administration of Bolton under the Bishop of Lichfield is confirmed by a record at Lichfield of the foundation of a Bolton prebend and vicarage in 1253. The succession of clergy in Bolton is registered from that time. A new Bolton Parish Church of St Peter was built c1420 and in 1541 the parish came within the Diocese of Chester and under the bishop at that cathedral.

Chapels of ease were built from the early 1500s in some outlying townships of Bolton. The name Chapeltown indicates the presence of a chapel of ease within the Parish of Bolton le Moors. On the opposite side of Turton Heights was a chapel of ease (Walmsley Chapel), on Cox Green Road at Dimple. Discoveries in the 20th century revealed an early Christian presence on the site of Walmsley Old Chapel and a Saxon burial ground was discovered in 1838 on the original site of Christ Church, Walmsley. Some writers have claimed an early medieval origin for Turton Chapel but the first contemporary record of its existence is dated 1523 when the first lords of the manor started to live in Turton. By this date, just prior to the English Reformation, the chapel had become a chapel of ease thought to be dedicated to St. Bartholomew the Apostle. It is also likely, although there is no record, that Walmsley Old Chapel may also have existed before the Reformation.

1.3 The English Reformation and break with Rome

Henry V111, acting largely from domestic motives, caused a break with Rome in the 1530s, and the creation of the Church of England. The rich monastic houses throughout England were one of the King's first targets for dissolution and confiscation of assets. A few of the abbey churches near large centres of population survived as cathedrals or parish churches, but most were demolished.

In 1534 parliament was pressurised into passing a series of Acts which effectively changed the old church into the Church of England with Henry as its supreme ruler. Anglicanism initially retained much of the structure of Roman Catholicism, both in terms of administration and liturgy. In time though, it became influenced by the ideas of Luther, Calvin and other Reformers.

Translation of the Bible into English, the introduction of the Book of Common Prayer, and the use of English rather than Latin in services were largely the initiatives of Thomas Cranmer, Archbishop of Canterbury, under Henry V111. The old clergy offices (prayers, psalms, etc.) of the monastic religious communities were adapted into set services for everyone. Church interiors changed, their appearance becoming less ornate and with less furniture. Stained glass in the windows was mostly replaced by plain glass, and church walls that had previously been decorated with paintings were often whitewashed.

The transition of the Church of England from Roman Catholic to a reformed church was not smooth. When Henry's daughter Mary, became Queen she restored the English church to papal supremacy. A devout Catholic, she sanctioned the persecution of Protestants, to such an extent that she earned the title '*Bloody Mary.*'

The Protestant Queen Elizabeth I, who succeeded Mary in 1558, implemented a compromise settlement, sufficiently broad to accommodate most Protestants and Catholics. The 39 Articles of Religion were established by a Convocation in the Church of England in 1563 under the Archbishop of Canterbury, Matthew Parker. They were intended as a statement of the position of the Church of England vis-à-vis the Roman Catholic Church and dissident Protestants. They highlighted the Anglican position with regard to Calvinism and the corruption of Catholic doctrine and teaching in the pre-Reformation period.

Following the Reformation, some of the clergy wanted a more severe break with Rome than was initially intended. Some of the Anglican rituals were not acceptable and a more simple interpretation of the Christian faith was sought. This was the origin of the puritan movement that developed in several ways. At first, puritans were content to work within the system and leave bishops in place; but purge the church of the *'Popery'* that had been left over by the political compromises of Elizabeth 1.

1.4 The Civil War and Commonwealth

Charles 1 (1600-49) favoured the elaborate and ritualistic High Anglican form of worship. William Laud, appointed Archbishop of Canterbury in 1633, insisted upon strict compliance to the tenets of the Church of England and vigorously supported the King's absolute rule. Laud also made extensive use of special courts to suppress opposition from puritans who regarded his High Church Liturgy as dangerously close to Roman Catholicism. The King's wife Henrietta Maria, a Roman Catholic, was allowed to practise her religion freely which caused some consternation amongst Protestants. Although Charles himself was high minded and devout, his religious policies were deeply divisive. His belief in the *'Divine Right of Kings'* (i.e. that the king could do no wrong), led to some uncompromising ideas on taxation and representation that caused a break with parliament and a disastrous civil war. The outcome was the defeat and execution of the King, the establishment of a republic and a victory for Puritanism.

During the Civil War and Commonwealth (1641-1660), conventional church government broke down, the traditional censorship ended and much debate on religious matters ensued. Various sects were able to emerge and assert their independence. Among these were the Presbyterians, Independents, Quakers, Baptists, etc. The Church in England passed through very turbulent times and many local churches were radically affected.

Presbyterianism represented the features of Protestantism emphasised by John Calvin (1509-64). Presbyterians were against hierarchical church government, holding that all clergy are equal and that church authority is vested not in individuals (like bishops) but in representative bodies composed of lay (ruling) elders and duly ordained (ruling and teaching) ministers. The Presbyterians were the largest body of dissenters in the mid-17th century.

Parliament, in 1646, mainly under the influence of Presbyterian members, approved a system of church government based on the *'Classis System'*. Lancashire was one of the few places where it was fully implemented due to the efforts of John Tilsley, Minister of Deane, near Bolton. It involved dividing the

County into nine *'Classis'* or church administrative districts each governed by a committee of clergy and lay elders without any bishops. Bolton-le-Moors Parish was included in the *'Second Classis'* together with the parishes of Deane, Radcliffe, Middleton, Bury and Rochdale. The system seems to have worked until it was abolished at the Restoration.

A new system of Presbyterian ecclesiastical organisation emerged in 1645 when Parliament replaced the Book of Common Prayer with the Directory of Public Worship. Other ordinances followed all intended to establish a Presbyterian form of worship. When the authority of parliament became complete, the whole Church adopted the Presbyterian system which remained until 1662. In this period, any remaining altars, raised communion tables, images, pictures and organs were removed from churches. From 1646 the offices of archbishop and bishop were abolished and their possessions invested in certain trusts. About 2000 Church of England ministers could not bring themselves to accept the new order and resigned or were removed from their livings.

Trustees were empowered to appoint commissioners '*able persons to survey premises*' and take charge of all related deeds and charters. Orders were given to sell lands and possessions, other than the burial grounds. Further, in 1649 it was enacted that the name, title, dignity, function and office of dean, sub-dean, chapter, and all other titles related to churches should be abolished. All lands and possessions belonging to these clergy were to be sold.

An '*Act Providing Maintenance for preaching ministers, and other pious use*' was passed, and a commission set up. The Lancashire Commission of 1650 followed, with the first inquisition held in Manchester in June of that year. Surveys followed on matters relating to churches, parsonages, schools, incumbents, patrons, salaries and parish needs. The Survey for Lancashire showed there were 63 parish churches and 118 chapels of ease in 1650 of which no less than 38 were without minister, chiefly for want of 'maintenance'.

Several of the Lancashire parishes were very large, and the commissioners wisely recommended their subdivision; whilst some of the chapels of ease were so far from their mother-church that it was thought desirable that they should become separate parish churches. Bolton-le-Moors was one such parish which contained five chapels: Turton, Walmsley, Bradshaw, Rivington and Blackrod. It was recommended following an official inquiry taken in Manchester in 1653 that Turton and Walmsley chapels were *'fit to be made parishes'* and to have their boundaries and precincts formally allotted and clearly defined to the benefit of the inhabitants resident in each area.

The surveys carried the signatures of ministers and lay people. At Bolton-le-Moors Church, Richard Goodwin, minister, and John Harper, pastor, were signatories for both the clergy and people. Both were regarded by the parishioners as men of integrity and Godly preaching ministers. As incumbents of the church, Harper and Goodwin's maintenance included the annual rents drawn from a mansion house, glebe lands in the large parish and six small cottages. At Deane (Dean) the signatories were John Tildesley (Tilsley) and Alex Horrocks.

1.5 The Restoration

To re-establish Anglicanism following the Restoration of Charles 11 in 1660, the Act of Uniformity was introduced in 1662 forcing all clergy to conform to the articles and liturgy of the Church of England, to adhere to the Book of Common Prayer, and subscribe to a declaration that there was no obligation lying on them from the oath of *'the Solemn League and Covenant'*. Those who refused were ejected from their livings and silenced; this included no less than 67 ministers of churches and chapels in Lancashire alone. The Act was particularly severe on a puritan area like Bolton and involved the ejection of Richard Goodwin, Vicar of Bolton, and five other clergymen from the parish. Two more statutes followed designed to suppress the rise in nonconformity by restricting preaching activities and banning covert meetings. These were the Conventicle Act of 1664 that restricted private religious meetings to five persons, and the Five Mile Act of 1665 that forbade dissenting clergy from living or coming within five miles of any corporate town or place where they had previously preached. The Acts led to much hardship as dissenting ministers were excluded from their calling and, in many cases, were condemned to a life of poverty. Some who fell foul of the penal laws, like John Bunyan, spent long periods in gaol. The restrictions did not achieve the desired effect and it was said that the established church '*gained neither in reputation or numbers.*'

Charles II in 1672, under his Declaration of Indulgence, tried to relax the laws against dissenters and Catholics. But parliament, fearing a covert attempt to reintroduce Roman Catholicism, forced him to withdraw and the penal laws remained. In 1688 James II attempted a similar initiative, which provoked an even more explosive reaction.

1.6 The Revolution of 1688

James II, a Roman Catholic, came to the throne in England in 1685 after Charles II, his brother, had died. He desired to rule despotically and to re-establish the Roman Catholic religion. The country grew increasingly restive and eventually parliament asked William of Orange, to take the crown together with his wife Mary, daughter of James II. William with his army invaded the country, the English army and people largely supported him and James II fled to Ireland. The event became known as the *'Glorious Revolution'* of 1688, because it attained its objective of maintaining Protestantism and the role of parliament without bloodshed. The Toleration Act followed a year later that allowed nonconformists to erect their own licensed chapels, but not Unitarians, Catholics or Jews, and Test Acts remained that excluded non Anglicans from public office. Not until the 19th century were all restrictions removed.

1.7 The Growth of Non-Conformist Churches

The latter part of the 17th and early 18th centuries became a period of great enthusiasm for nonconformists. The changes of official attitudes were a signal for a spate of activity in chapel building. Most chapels were built as preaching houses and as such were not primarily concerned with satisfying ritualistic requirements of worship. For example, the almost universally adopted central position of the pulpit at the focal point was and still is a feature in nonconformist buildings, which starkly contrasts with pre-Reformation church layouts where the altar has a prominent central position.

Nonconformist attitudes in Turton were influenced largely from Bolton, once reputed to be *'The Geneva of the North'*, although the north side of Turton was to a lesser extent influenced from Blackburn and Darwen. Turton retained several nonconformist traditions including: Independents, Presbyterians, and Quakers. Other nonconformist churches such as Baptists developed in the mid 17th century but none became established in Turton. Methodism followed in the 18th century as a result of the activities of John and Charles Wesley.

1.8 The Independents and Congregationalists

The Congregationalists or Independents were originally known as Brownists, after Robert Browne, who in 1580 asserted the principle that a local congregation is completely autonomous under God and should not submit to any outside, human authorities such as Presbyterian elders or Episcopalian bishops. Oliver Cromwell himself was an Independent and his army were mainly of this persuasion. The essential problem for the Commonwealth was that, although the army could control the country, the Independents could never get enough of their supporters into a free parliament to confirm them in legitimate power. Eventually the Independents evolved into the Congregational Church more recently known as the United Reformed Church.

By the beginning of the 18th century, there were Lancashire dissenting ministers and congregations who were not conscious of being distinctively Presbyterian or Independent but as the 18th century took its course, clearer distinctions appeared among the dissenters. The majority of dissenting congregations in Lancashire became Unitarian but often retained the title Presbyterian. The congregations that remained Independent, and likewise the minority that had seceded from Unitarian congregations, organised themselves as Congregational chapels.

1.9 Presbyterians and Unitarians

John Biddle (1615-62), the founder of English Unitarianism, understood the Greek text of the New Testament which convinced him that the orthodox *'Doctrine of the Holy Trinity'* was not of scriptural origin. He published his *'Unitarian Convictions in 12 Arguments'* drawn out of the scriptures. When the existence of this paper was first made known to the magistrates in 1645 Biddle was imprisoned, as he was frequently thereafter. His *'12 Arguments'* was suppressed and burnt publicly in 1647. Upon the publication of his two-fold catechism in 1654 he was tried for his life but received from Cromwell a sentence of banishment to the Scilly Isles. Returning in 1658 he taught and preached until 1662 afterwards being again thrown into prison where he died .His followers were called Biddelians, Socinians or Unitarians. The Unitarians believe that God exists only in one person, and in the *'Fatherhood of God'* and the *'Brotherhood of Man'*. They give a pre-eminent position to Jesus Christ as a religious teacher, while denying his deity.

The first English Unitarian congregation was founded in London in 1774 by Theophilus Lindsey who previously had been an Anglican clergyman. The scientist and dissenting minister Joseph Priestley 1733-1804 influenced Unitarian ministers by his scriptural rationalism and materialist determinism. Although Unitarianism began as a scripturally orientated movement, by the mid 19th century it was transformed into a religion of reason. By the Victorian period English Presbyterians had largely mutated into Unitarians.

1.10 Quakers

The Quakers (also known as The Religious Society of Friends) is an English sect founded c.1644-1660, known for their radical social theology. Quakerism had a major impact during the Commonwealth. After the Restoration the sect redirected itself and its effort to a more internal individual enlightenment. The sect was based on the personal insights of George Fox (1624-91). Between 1643 and 1647 Fox went through his own religious conversion to find the *'Inner Light'* within him.

From his experiences Fox developed a new set of religious values, possibly influences by early Baptist writings, based on the idea that all men were equal in the spirit of God. Fox gathered small groups of religious converts that formed the early basis for his *'Meetings of Friends'*.

Fox was imprisoned in Nottingham in 1649, arrested under the Blasphemy Law of 1650 and sent to prison at Derby. He spoke out against the vain and worldly practises he saw in society and voiced his views on the *'Coming Day of Judgement'*. By 1652 a major evangelical effort had begun to spread across England. Groups of Quaker ministers and preachers were canvassing towns and villages broadcasting the new Quaker message. Women membership was encouraged and contributed to the spread of the movement. Early Quakers were often called the *'People of God'* or just *'Friends'*.

Quakerism before 1660 was a political, social and religious movement, which rejected the privileged structure of English society. Quakers envisaged a new society based on their own religious views of all Godly members having the same *'Internal Light or Spirit of Christ'*. They believed in the *'Universal Salvation'* or *'Free Will'* for all men, rather than the predestination of Calvinism. All men could thus be saved from sin by the *'Indwelling Light'*.

Quakerism had a strong anti-clerical bent rejecting all ordinations and administrative structures. No sacramental or ceremonial worship was to detract the individual from the *'Inner Light of God'*. Quaker Meetings were a time to wait in silence to contemplate God. Having no official clergy, lay preachers including women, could officiate at Meetings.

Quakers also rejected most of the civil and legal authorities and their laws. Public oaths, and the payment of tithes to the state church or its ministers were considered illegal. They often spoke very harshly to non-Quaker groups and had a habit of disrupting their services. This radical theology brought Quakerism into direct conflict with the state and the church authorities. Quakers had their own distinctive dress and hat styles and a certain style of speech was assumed. Their exacting rules prevented them from growing in numbers, notably their insistence that members who married non-Quakers be expelled. Young men and women were advised not to *'let their minds go out to such as were not of their sect'*. This general practice was dropped as late as 1863.

1.11 Baptists

The Baptists were founded by John Smyth, a refugee from England, in Amsterdam in 1609. They believed in baptism for believers by total immersion and repudiated infant baptism. Before the Civil War they had divided into two groups, the 'General Baptists' who believed in general redemption of believers and the 'Particular Baptists' who believed in redemption only for particular believers. In 1770 a *'New Connection'* group was formed while the *'Old Connection'* joined with the Unitarians. Late in the 19th century the New Connection and Particular Baptists joined together under the influence of the Baptist Union. There were no traditional Baptist churches recorded in Turton.

1.12. Anglicans

After the Restoration the Church of England, with the king as its ruler, enjoyed a unique position as the established church. Its bishops sat in the House of Lords, it had its own courts to administer parts of the law, it virtually controlled the universities (Oxford and Cambridge) and, under the Test Acts, entry into parliament, public office or the professions was confined to its members. This situation remained until well into the nineteenth century.

During the 19th century, divisions emerged among Anglicans in the form of three main parties. The Evangelical or Low Church maintained the church's Protestant character; the Anglo-Catholic or High Church stressed continuity with the pre-Reformation church, while Central Churchmanship occupied the middle ground. Although some churches neatly fit into these divisions many do not and hence there are no two churches that are exactly alike.

Anglican church services largely enable the congregation to share fully in the services. Since the Reformation several prayer books have been duly authorised from the traditional to the modern form. Briefly, the first Book of Common Prayer dated 1549 was issued with the first Act of Uniformity. This was revised in 1552, again in 1662 and again in 1928.

In Bolton the parish church and various chapels of ease, having been purged of puritan influences after the Reformation, continued to serve for a while. Eventually however the whole traditional parish structure in Lancashire was found to be too limited to cater for the greatly increased population resulting from the industrial revolution. Additional churches had to be built in the parish from the mid 18th century. The Bishopric of Manchester was formed in 1847 and Bolton became part of that See. The parish of Bolton-le-Moors was too large and accordingly was divided into several new ones, some based on the old chapels of ease. In Turton two new parishes were based on St Anne's, Turton and Christ Church, Walmsley. In Bolton the mediaeval parish church continued in use until c1865 when it had to be replaced by a more capacious structure capable of serving a vastly increased population.

1.13 Methodists

John Wesley (1703-91) was an Anglican minister and theologian who established the Methodist movement in 1739. Wesley, along with others, took to itinerant field preaching and the founding of a religious society that can claim to be the first widely successful evangelical movement in the country. Methodism, originally a movement to invigorate the Church of England from within, eventually drifted away, because the institutional rigidity of the Anglican church did not allow it to respond to evangelisation. Methodism in its several forms became popular in the new towns thrown up by the industrial revolution, where the established church and the 'old dissenters' had become too exclusive to provide for the growing working population.

Wesley had taken the trouble to visit and preach in these areas and to some extent the geographical distribution of Methodist communities is a reflection of his travels. The original church became known as the Wesleyan Methodist Church but schisms, caused in part by lay members wanting to govern their own societies, led numerous factions to break away at different times including the Methodist New Connection (1797), the Primitive Methodists (1811), the Bible Christians (1815), the Protestant Methodists (1828), and the United Methodist Free Church (1857). The Bible Christians, Methodist New Connection and United Methodist Free Church combined in 1907 to form the United Methodist Church and this became amalgamated with the Primitives and some Wesleyans in 1932. Still separate were the Wesleyan Reform Union and the Independent Methodists, the latter being mainly confined to Lancashire.

The Methodists were essentially linked to a changing social structure and their buildings reflect this. The greater proportion of nonconformist chapels were built of good local materials, some resembling Anglican buildings, some furnished in a 'farm-house' style; while others, particularly those regarded as mission stations, were often more austere. Some were even initially built of corrugated-iron. The advent of Methodism gave men (and later women) of all classes not only the opportunity to worship, but to organise their own affairs. Ministers, itinerant preachers, deacons and elders came from all levels of society and reflected every degree of education. Men emerged from a background of manual labour to become preachers and leaders of congregations and educated themselves in order to do so. Out of such circumstances came new demands for mass elementary education and literacy, hence the importance of the Sunday School movement. Chapel building became almost a mania and there are instances of chapels being erected almost single-handed by new converts to the faith. Men devoted their lives and fortunes to the provision of chapels, many built outside a town and village centre in the rural highways and by-ways. Turton had several such chapels, some still functioning today.

John Wesley visited Bolton more than 24 times between 1748 and 1788. He preached at Bolton's market cross on Sunday 28th August 1748 to a vast number of people, many of them utterly wild. He was heckled, threatened with removal from where he stood and stoned. When travelling between Bolton and Darwen (c1780) he stopped to address workmen who were re-building Wayoh Bridge. He preached in Wayoh Lodge Farm Yard and at Holden Fold, now submerged by Wayoh Reservoir. Prior to 1932 there were at least two different Methodist traditions in Turton: the Wesleyans and the Primitives. Some of Turton's Methodist Chapels closed after this date; others are still in use.

1.14 Roman Catholics

Executions were carried out in the 16th century for the crime of harbouring priests. An Act of 1606 forbad recusants (Catholics who refused to conform to the established church) from holding any kind of public office in England. The relatively small number of Catholics affected included a few families of Lancashire gentry who retained the Catholic faith down the centuries. Throughout the 17th century many recusants were *'overcharged with debt'* for having to re-purchase their land and pay heavy recusancy fines uncollected since Elizabethan times. After the Restoration Roman Catholics were still persecuted for practising their religion and excluded from public office.

The religious state of Lancashire county and its gentry in the mid 1600's is still being researched but it is probably true to say that Lancashire was more sharply divided in religion than any other English county. Lancashire had a high proportion of Roman Catholics in the northern and western parts of the county, although the Salford Hundred and particularly Bolton and Manchester were strongly puritan, due, it is thought, to the strong influence of the textile trade in these areas which facilitated the spread of religious ideas current in London.

After the Restoration, Roman Catholics were subject to much the same restrictions as the nonconformists. However two Catholic Relief Acts in 1778 and 1791 and the Catholic Emancipation Act of 1829 restored freedom of worship and education for Catholics, although they were still regarded with suspicion for some time afterwards. Throughout the late 19th century there was a significant increase in the Roman Catholic population in England, largely brought about by immigration and inter-marriage.

Numbers increased in industrial centres like Bolton and Darwen, aided by the many Irish employed on canal and railway construction. Salford Diocese, which included Bolton and Turton, was one of the first to be established when the Catholic hierarchy of England & Wales was founded in 1850.

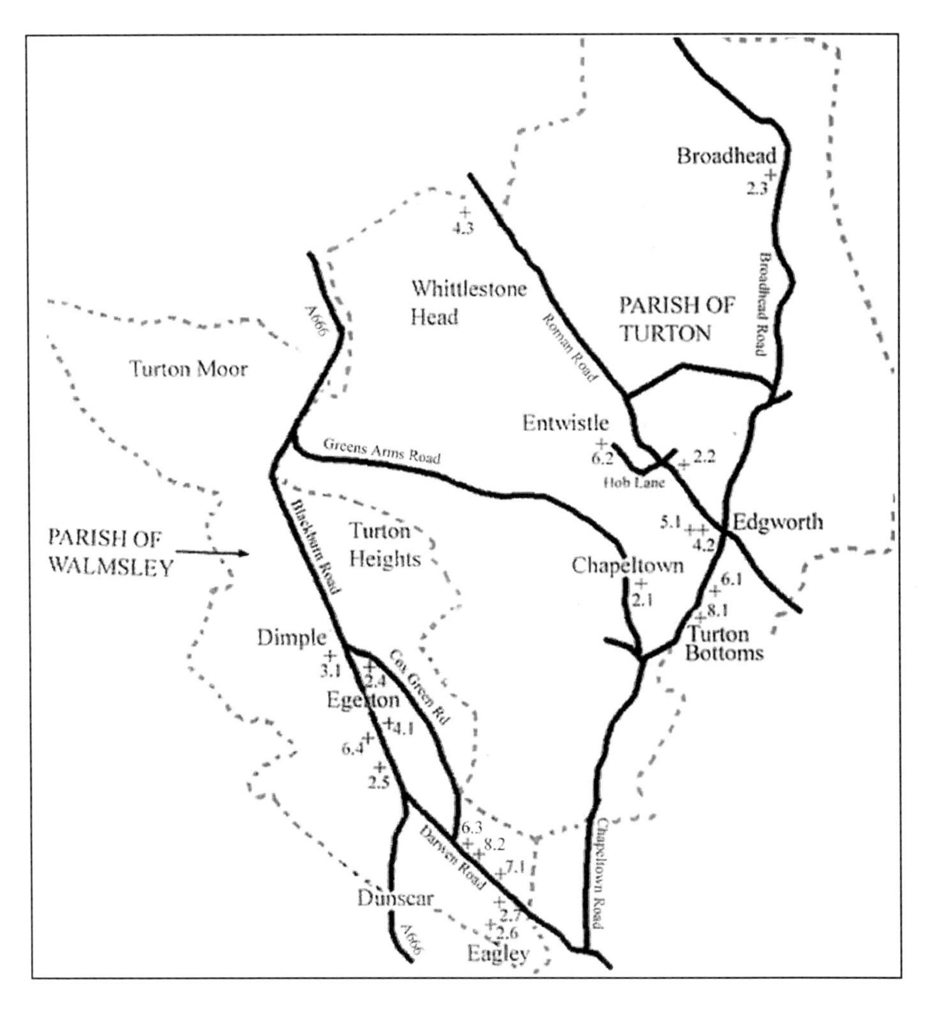

Map showing Turton Parish and Walmsley Parish boundaries (broken lines) and the location of churches or chapels numbered according to the chapter and section in which they are described in this book as follows:-

2.1	St Anne's Church, Chapeltown	4.3	Whittlestone Head Chapel, Entwistle
2.2	St James's Church, Hob Lane	5.1	Edgworth Meeting House
2.3	Broadhead Mission	6.1	Edgworth Methodist Church
2.4	Walmsley Old Chapel	6.2	Entwistle Methodist Chapel
2.5	Christ Church Walmsley	6.3	Birtenshaw Methodist Church
2.6	Eagley Schools	6.4	Egerton Methodist Church
2.7	St Andrew's Church, Bromley Cross	7.1	Cornerstone Baptist Church
3.1	Walmsley Unitarian Chapel	8.1	St Aldhelm's Church, Edgworth
4.1	Egerton Congregational Chapel	8.2	St John's Church, Bromley Cross
4.2	Edgworth Congregational Church		

CHAPTER 2 ANGLICANS IN TURTON

2.1 St Anne's Church, Chapeltown

The Chapelry of Turton may have existed since the time of Roger de Poictou (Pitou), builder of Bolton Parish Church, but there is no exact date recording its founding. The first lords of the manor who lived in Turton and therefore had need of a chapel were the Orrells who built Turton Tower c.1430. It is thought that a separate village chapel may have been built in the late 1400s when 'private' chapel building by local worthies such as the Orrells was popular. Such chapels were referred to as '*free chapels*', and over the centuries Turton Chapel was known as '*Turton Free Chapel*', emphasising its ownership by the lords of the manor. By 1523 the chapel was *'in the gift of Ralf (Rauff) Orrell, Lord of the Manor of Turton'*, and the incumbent was James Anderton. A Lord of the Manor in this period had authority to appoint or remove an incumbent. As the chapel existed before the Reformation it was possibly an endowed chantry chapel where confessions were heard and mass was celebrated.

After the Reformation, the chapel continued as a chapel of ease in the Parish of Bolton-le-Moors. In 1628, Humphrey Chetham, the philanthropist, purchased the Manor of Turton from William Orrell which included the chapel (or *aisle appurtenan to Turton).* The chapel was rebuilt in 1630 and Humphrey Chetham bequeathed money in 1655 for: '*an oaken bookcase containing 45 volumes of works of theology to be chained fast for the use of the incumbent and the few literate parishioners'*. In 1978 the bookcase was moved to Turton Tower.

During the Commonwealth, the incumbent at Chapeltown in 1650 was James Livesey, known as a *'painful Godly orthodox minister'* who was maintained by free gifts and contributions from his congregation. Michael Bristow (too much of a dissenter) was ousted from Turton Chapel by Humphrey Chetham but managed to continue at Walmsley Old Chapel for a few years. Although the Chethams had supported parliament, they remained Anglican throughout the Commonwealth. There does not seem to be any record of nonconformists breaking away from Turton Chapel after the Restoration.

The second Humphrey Chetham was instrumental in obtaining Queen Anne's Bounty (a state supplement to the incomes of the poorer Anglican clergy) in 1717. The chapel was not licensed for weddings at the time, there was no resident incumbent and it was served by curates from Bolton Parish Church until about 1705. In 1779 the chapel was again rebuilt and is recorded as being a long low building with mullioned windows, leaded panes, and a gallery accessible by an outside staircase. This chapel, and probably its predecessor, was built to the south-west of the present church.

For over 200 years, Turton Fair was held within the Chapel Fields, its origins rooted in an all-night service commemorating the patron saint's feast day, 24th August, with eating, drinking, trading and bartering. Part of a poem by a Mr William Sheldrake sold in Bolton by Benjamin Jackson in 1789 describes the chapel service before the fair starts:

'Near two full hours before meridian day,
The Chapel's throng'd by people bent to pray;
When praying's o'er the heav'nly man begins
To warn his hearers 'gainst presumptuous sins'.

In 1837 Turton was made an ecclesiastical parish in its own right, following the increase in local population, and a larger building became necessary. A notice appeared in the Bolton Chronicle April 7th 1838 and in the Bolton Free Press at a similar date:

TURTON NEW CHURCH
TO STONE MASONS AND STONE GETTERS
TO BE LET BY TICKET

At the Cheetham's Arms Inn, Chapel Town, on Monday, the 9th of April next at Twelve o'clock
The Masons' Work and Getting of the Stone for a new Church, at Turton.
The Plans, Specifications, and Specimens of the work may be seen at Mr Nathan Holt's [Parish Clerk] *Chapel House, Chapel Town, any day after the 28th of March. The Carpenters', Joiners', and other developments of the works will be let at a future period, of which due notice will be given.*

Turton, March 22nd. 1838.

The old chapel was demolished in 1840/41 and the new church, still in use, was built on an adjoining site. The church is dedicated to St Anne and was consecrated on October 2nd , 1841, by the Bishop of Chester. A brass plaque at the back of the church commemorates the occasion.

The church was associated with an ancient school erected by the Chetham family before 1716, probably the same one that Samuel Chetham gave £100 to in 1717, the interest from which clothed five boys. By 1828 the school had some 28 scholars, both boys and girls. The old school eventually proved to be too small and in 1871 was replaced by St Anne's National School.

The Ogden-Spencer family provided Turton's clergy from 1761 to 1899. Amos Ogden was incumbent 1762-1815, followed in 1815 by his grandson James

Spencer Snr who served up to 1859. From 1859, James's son and curate, James Jnr. (also known by his initials as J O K) was incumbent to 1879, when he suddenly died and was succeeded by his younger brother, John William Spencer, who served at Turton until 1899. The Spencer family grave and stone is in the churchyard and is thought to be sited over the altar of the old chapel.

A '*new clock for Turton Church*' was recorded in the Bolton Chronicle on August 20th, 1859. The clock, with 4 dials, was installed in the tower at a cost of £100 and Mr Lee of Turton was entrusted with the manufacture of it. The church tower also houses one bell, which was cast and probably hung in 1859.

Considerable damage was done to the church by lightning on July 4th, 1871 when the '*electric fluid*' struck one of the tower pinnacles, hurling it to the ground and dislodged one of the coping stones, weighing about 2 cwt. The latter fell through the church roof onto the organ which was completely shattered. The stone penetrated the floor of the gallery wrecking the pews beneath.

The organ and choir stalls, originally located in the west gallery, were moved to their present position in the chancel organ chamber in 1890/91. In 1898 old enclosed box-pews were replaced with seats which are still used today and the galleries were re-fronted.

In 1888 the chancel was enlarged and re-furbished by Robert Knowles of Swinton Old Hall, as an inscribed brass in the chancel bears witness. In the same year an eye-catching marble reredos was erected in memory of Robert Knowles by his three sons and a new enlarged high altar enclosing the old one was constructed..

A silver flagon, chalice, and paten are inscribed: *'The gift of Humy. Chetham, Esq. To Turton Chappel, 1748*. (The donor was the great great nephew of Humphrey Chetham, 1580-1653.) In 1883 a silver chalice was given by a few parishioners and friends, to supplement the communion plate already presented. The chancel oak panelling and screens were donated in 1924 by George and Rose Walker, and the Rood Screen was donated in 1927 by Robert Kenyon, owner of Horrobin Bleachworks. The brass eagle lectern was given in 1907 by Alice Walker of Spring Vale Weaving Mill in memory of her father, the Rev'd J O K Spencer, incumbent of the parish from 1859 to 1879. The marble pulpit, designed to tone-in with the reredos, was installed in 1919 as a war memorial and carries plaques listing Turton men killed in both World Wars.

The font of Caen Stone on alabaster columns was presented in 1899 by the Rev'd J W Spencer in memory of his brother George A F Spencer and carries the inscription:-

9781904974314

Turton Old Chapel rebuilt in 1779, demolished in 1840.

St Anne's east window and chancel: 1902.

St Anne's first May Queen event at Turton CE School: c1950.

'To the Glory of God and in memory of G.A.F. Spencer, this font is given by his brother J.W. Spencer MA, Vicar of Turton, at the close of his 40th year of his ministry, 20 years of which were spent at Turton --Trinity Sunday 1899.

A side altar, and a desk were donated by the congregation of the former Broadhead Mission in Edgworth. Among the windows, the magnificent stained glass East Window was donated in 1886 by the widow of Kay Knowles. The two windows on the north side were donated by parishioners. On the south side there are three windows, one in memory of James Kay and his wife of Turton Tower. St Anne's celebrated its 150th anniversary in 1991 and remains active today.

As the parish boundary of St Anne's Church, Chapeltown was nearly 18 miles long, it was decided in the mid-19th century to establish two mission stations. One in Hob Lane in an old school which eventually was replaced by St James's Church. The other was Broadhead Mission, built in 1855 in Edgworth, about three miles from St Anne's.

2.2 St James's Church, Hob Lane

From around 1880 services in the Hob Lane area were held in an old stone school in School Lane, traditionally called Hob Lane School, built in the early 1800s and now demolished. The school had originally no direct connection with the Church having been established by the nonconformists as a non-denominational school.

On February 2nd 1898 the Bishop of Manchester, after an official visit to Hob Lane, recommended the site to a commission, set up in 1901, to consider the needs of the Bolton Deanery. A meeting of clergy and lay people was held in St Anne's School on February 11th, 1903 '*To appoint suitable Hob Lane Mission Church or School gentlemen to act as building committee.*' It was decided that the building would be best built near Hob Lane rather than on an alternative site near to the White Horse and that a school church would be preferable to a church. At a meeting the following month Mr Abraham Morris was thanked for the '*piece of land, near Hob Lane lying between Cherry Tree Cottages and the next row of houses, for the building of a Church*'. On August 16th, 1904 the architect was requested to present plans and obtain tenders for building, the eventual contract going to Messrs Martin Brothers of Turton.

Foundation Stones were laid at a ceremony performed in brilliant weather on 13 May 1905 by Henry Seymoor Hoare Esq and Colonel Sir Lees Knowles Bart MP Behind each stone was placed a bottle containing local newspapers and a number of coins. The Bishop of Manchester dedicated the church during the first

St James's, Hob Lane in 2006.

A Sunday School nativity play held at St James's in the early 1970s.

service on November 17th, 1905 at 7.00pm in the presence of a large number of people including the Rural Dean of Bolton.

The church was built on two levels, the worship centre above and a social hall, kitchen, and boiler house below. It was built from bricks from the Black Hill Brickworks close to Entwistle Railway Station. It had a tile glazed border of 3 feet, 6 inches in the top room, pitch pine beams, and only the ceiling plastered in the downstairs room.

For many years several old local families were stalwarts at the church, including the Morris and the Entwistle families, some were local farmers, others worked at Know Mill or the Black Hill Brickworks.

The First Anniversary Sermons Sunday was May 6th, 1906. Each year following, processions were held in May starting with a short indoor service followed by a walk around the White Horse junction, Blackburn Road, Hob Lane, and Entwistle. The Sunday School children headed the procession. It was traditional for the little girls (little singers) to be trained to sing two hymns, one for the afternoon service, the other for Evensong. All in white dresses wearing a veil they would form an important part of the day.

Church organisations in 1906 included a choir and a well-attended Sunday School. The annual outing for the choristers and teachers was by train to Waddington. A Men's Club, formed before WW1, ran until the end of WW2. They had a billiard table in the basement and the first annual social of the Men's Club was held on April 28th, 1906. About 20 friends of the members were present and after tea-dancing, the Burton Bijou Orchestra played a good programme of dance music. The Club had an average attendance of 30 in 1906 and was very much appreciated by the men of Hob Lane district during the cold winter evenings. St James' centenary was reached in 2005 and it is still providing services and social events within the parish of St Anne.

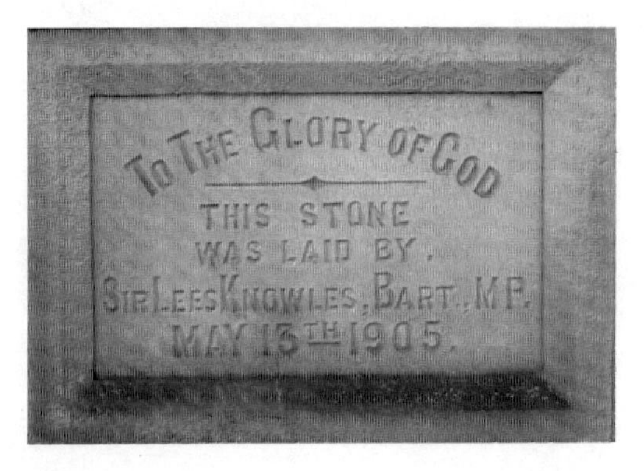

Foundation stone at St James's, laid by Sir Lees Knowles on 13th May, 1905.

2.3 Broadhead Mission

On the northern side of St Anne's Parish a daughter church known as the Broadhead Mission existed for 140 years. Built and opened in 1836, it was used as a day school in the first few years as well as for regular worship and social events.

At the time it was built, the Bishop of Chester was encouraging the inhabitants of rural valleys in the diocese to build mission churches. When one considers the bleakness of the Broadhead valley, even today, the local farmers, residents and others deserve much praise for providing the means and driving force to build this chapel. '*The Mission*', as it became known, provided a local place for worship and secular instruction for these people and their children.

Records show that even when winter blizzards swept across the moors the vicar always seemed to successfully struggle through to the Mission from Chapeltown. For many decades services were regularly held once a month, usually at full-moon, on Sunday afternoons. The choir consisted of local boys and girls mainly from the Broadhead valley, and the organist for many years commuted from Bromley Cross. Local taxi owner, Edgworth's George Knowles, also the village greengrocer, invariably '*ferried*' the vicar and the organist to and from the Mission. The vicar was known to occasionally pop-in the nearby Toby Inn to '*tipple a noggin*' en route. The inn landlord was then part of the local community, in sympathy with the Mission's cause, and often attended services. One exception to the '*ferry by taxi*' routine was during a short period when the vicar pedalled his bike between St Anne's and the Mission.

Well remembered is one very cold Sunday when the Mission's heating system failed and the service of Holy Communion was held for the small congregation in the home of a local couple. Originally, heating was supplied by a coke stove placed in the middle of the building with a pipe through the roof. It was always lit well in time for social events, usually held on Saturday evenings, and kept 'stoked-up' so that the room would be warm for worshippers the following day. Eventually electric heating was installed.

The place became famous and people came from far and wide to attend. At harvest services, lavish displays of fruit and vegetables were mounted on the window sills, down the aisle, and on the altar. Ample provisions were brought to the Mission by horse & cart; to such an extent that a sale of the produce was needed after the event. Everyone was invited to 'buy back' the perishable fruits and vegetables as well as the canned produce. Boxes of apples, bags of home-grown potatoes, and coal, were gratefully given and later sold to raise much needed funds for the Mission.

Broadhead Mission with a belfry in 1935. The group of people on the right include 12 years old George Winward, a life-long member of the Mission.

The Mission converted to a private residence named 'Mission House': 2008.

Maintenance of the building was always willingly carried out by the local people and it remained in a good state of repair. In the 1920s farmers and others helped to build a new pitch-pine roof which still exists today. A local family built the vestry. The Mission never had its own water supply. Members used to go to the Toby Inn with milk cans to fill with water for brewing tea and washing-up at social events. Electricity was installed from the time it was available by poles and cables within the Broadhead valley.

On Saturday nights in the winter months, on dates nearest to the full moon when it was relatively light for walking, and sometimes swinging a storm lamp, many local people attended the whist drives and dances. These events provided enjoyable social evenings and attracted people from miles around.

From its erection in 1836 to its closure in 1975 the Mission was continually used for worship and social life. Its demise occurred because the local farming community diminished, more residents had the means to travel, and there was a general decline in church-going.

Money from the sale of the building perpetuates the Mission's memory at St Anne's Church where the Broadhead Room provides a lovely addition which has proved adaptable and useful to the present community. Also certain items of the mission's furniture including the altar are now used in St Anne's Church.

2.4 Walmsley Old Chapel

Christ Church Walmsley, Walmsley Unitarian Chapel and Egerton Congregational Church all have their roots in an earlier mediaeval chapel built on the old Bolton to Blackburn Highway, now Cox Green Road, near Dimple. The site of the Old Chapel was about one mile north of the present Christ Church and about 100 yards east of the present Bolton to Darwen Road (A666).

Excavations on the site of the Old Chapel by Colonel Slater of Dunscar in 1905 revealed the foundations of some very old buildings at three levels. At the top level was a cross with one long arm, under this was a foundation with an apse, and below this was an equal sided cross which is nearly always Saxon in design and would date this finding to that period.

The remains of the Old Chapel at the end of the 19th century included ruined walls standing two to three feet high, from which the outline of the original building could be traced. At that time a few gravestones overgrown with grass also remained on the site, the oldest bearing the date 1750 and the most recent, belonging to the Kays of Turton, 1858.

The site of Walmsley Old Chapel on Cox Green Road behind the stone wall.
The Old Chapel House is in the background: 2006.

Ruins of the old chapel among trees in the left centre of the view: 1992.

The date when the Old Chapel was first erected is not known, but it is recorded as a chapel of ease to Bolton Parish Church in 1500 and a chapel erected in the early years of the 16th century must have been consecrated to the services of the Catholic Church, later known as the 'Old Religion'. Documentary evidence in the '*Inventories of Church Goods*' 1552 records '*Itm att Walmsley Chapel, a Chales, a Bell and other Ornametes for a p'ste'* [priest], meaning the chapel had a priest's chalice, a bell, and a few ornaments. According to a Visitation List of 1563 there was a curate attached to the chapel but this entry is erased in 1565. In the Turton enclosure dated the 20th May 1582 and executed by W Orrell Esq., Walmsley Chapel is mentioned in the description of the '*Boundaries of the Common Land then appointed and set out*'.

In the late 16th century the building had a capacity to accommodate about fifty persons and the first known curate, c1594, was the Rev'd Joshua Hill. Hill was the means of converting Alice Critchlaw, the mother of Oliver Heywood, who was born at Longworth, near Walmsley Chapel, in 1594. Her son writes that she '*was as careles, carnal and froward as any til she was about 19 years of age, at which time it pleased god to take to himselfe her gracious mother, whom she tenderly affected, and for whose death she made excessiue sorrow.*' At this time (1613) he further says '*there lived a godly young minister at the place, one Mr Joshua Hill, whom the Lord used as an instrument to open her blind eyes.*' The Rev'd John Harrison followed Hill at Walmsley from c.1635. He was the son of a Wigan gentleman, of good fortune, of the '*puritan stamp*', and university trained. His relationship with the Heywood family was quite close. From Walmsley Harrison is thought to have moved to Ashton-u-Lyne, where in 1642 he signed the '*Protestation*', an undertaking to maintain and defend the Protestant religion, adopted by parliament on May 3rd, 1641 and widely signed. He was described in an autobiography as one of the three men '*most deeply engaged*' for establishing Presbyterianism in Lancashire, and was one of the Lancashire ministers who signed the '*Harmonious Consent of 1648: a testimony to our Solemn League and Covenant, as also against the Errors, Heresies, and Blasphemies of the time and the Toleration thereof.*' Harrison was ejected in 1662, died in 1670 and was buried in the chancel at Ashton. Harrison was followed at Walmsley by the Rev'd Thomas Pyke c1640 but by 1646 had left to become minister at Radcliffe where he signed "The Consent" in 1648 and was ejected from there in 1662. Walmsley's next cleric was the Rev'd James Smith who ministered between 1647 and March 1648. Smith was regarded as '*a very honest man, of good life style and conversation*'.

It will be evident from the foregoing that the earlier ministers were mainly puritan and the long line was to continue for some years. The minister following James Smith, the Rev'd Michael Briscoe, was well known in the mid 1600s as a pillar of Lancashire nonconformity. Briscoe was born about 1619, educated at Trinity

College, Dublin and settled at Walmsley at about 29 years of age. There is some doubt as to whether Briscoe first went to Turton Chapel, and whether he was in sole charge, or ministered at both places simultaneously. It is thought possible that Briscoe went from Turton Chapel to Walmsley about 1652 after a quarrel with the Chetham family. Briscoe, an Independent cleric, had such unpopular and unacceptable views that he was locked out of Walmsley Chapel in 1654. These were the times when the Presbyterians and the Independents were competing with each other for supremacy, and Briscoe's Independency coupled with poor financial prospects caused him to leave Walmsley about 1654. There is some doubt about this date of his departure as it is elsewhere recorded that he was ejected from the living in 1662.

During the 17th century, the Old Chapel was the scene of much congregational division. There were those of the Anglican tradition, on the one hand, and worshippers with strong puritan leanings on the other, both claiming the right to use the chapel. During the Commonwealth period (1648 to 1660) the puritan party itself split into two rival factions; Presbyterians, and the Independents.

Humphrey Chetham provided books for the Old Chapel at Walmsley as well as for Turton Chapel and Bolton Parish Church before he died in 1653. Baines in his History of the County of Lancaster records: '*Inquisition taken at Manchester 1650. Boulton, a Parish Church, Mansion House on Glebe Lands belonging. There are five Chapels in Boulton Parish, Turton Chapel and Walmsley Chapel are fit to be made parishes*'.

After the Restoration, the puritans of Walmsley were not allowed to worship in the chapel or their homes. For fear of persecution and under cover of night, they used to meet secretly in a wild and lonely spot named Yearnsdale Holmes to worship. Although the situation eased slightly over time it was not until 1689 that greater freedom of worship was allowed and dissenters were then able to register buildings for public worship.

Following the departure of Briscoe there were no regular ministers for some years, according to The Victoria County History of Lancashire. Later however, following the issuing of the short lived *'Declaration of Indulgence in 1672'* a licence was issued to Thomas Key to be a Presbyterian teacher in the house of Francis Norbury of Entwistle, a place about a mile and a half from the Chapel. Although the Indulgence was withdrawn within a year, Key's ministry seems to have continued until about 1684. In November 1687 Charles Sager, an Independent, became minister before later imprisonment at Lancaster.

Relief came in 1689 with the Toleration Act. The Presbyterians of Walmsley now used the Chapel alternately with the Anglicans, although, this was strongly opposed by the Curate of Turton, the Rev'd H Lawson, who even enlisted the help of their landlords to try to force them to conform to the established church. In the year 1710 the Rev'd Lawson wrote to James Milne, Presbyterian minister from 1706, reprimanding him for christening children in the chapel. He also tried to convert the Presbyterians to his own way of thinking and worshipping. In the early 18th century James Milne urged the Presbyterians to build their own chapel at Dimple and withdraw from Walmsley Old Chapel. In 1710 they licensed a room from Evan Dewhurst in a house on the site of the present Globe Inn. This served until their own chapel was built in 1713.

The Anglicans now had sole use of the Old Chapel. In 1755 the Rev'd James Folds (Parson Folds), was appointed Lecturer to Bolton Parish Church and Curate of Walmsley Chapel. Many stories are told of the humorous sayings and doings of this witty and eccentric character. A story runs that whilst serving the curacy at Walmsley the old parson had reached the uppermost step of his pulpit for Sabbath duty, when a goose, which by some means had hobbled thither before him, was found apparently content with its elevation, *'Come thee out!'* said the preacher, *'one's a plenty'*. In 1771 the chapel was rebuilt, much smaller than the original, cruciform in structure, and benched for seating.

The Rev'd Lowther Grisdale took charge of the chapel in 1825 and on June 6th, 1826 the Rev'd James Slade (Canon Slade) wrote asking about the size and the accommodation afforded in the chapel. Grisdale replied that it was capable of accommodating 130 people seated on pews and was 32 ft long by 24 ft wide. There is a record of disputes between two local families about the use of the double pews. There were 12 single pews 9ft 4ins x 4ft 7ins and four double pews 9ft 4ins x 5ft 2ins. The top of the clerk's desk was 4 ft high, and the top of the pulpit 8 feet. In this period, income was derived from lands in Harwood and Over Darwen together with Queen Anne's Bounty. The Trustees in 1828 were: The Rev'd James Slade, the Rev'd Lowther Grisdale, Mr George Slater of the Holmes (a local industrialist), R Chadwick, Thos Appleton and Wm Howarth.

Grisdale started procuring funding for rebuilding a larger chapel on the same site, but after much deliberation, it was decided to build on a new site. Grisdale was helped in his endeavours by Mr George Slater, a Warden of the Old Chapel from 1835-1839 and who later became the first Warden at Christ Church. Although the Old Chapel was demolished in 1840 the site with a burial ground was preserved. Around the Year 1915 the Slater family paid for iron railings to enclose the burial ground. These were erected by teachers and members of Walmsley Sunday School. The iron gate was from an old door at G & J Slater's Bleachworks at Dunscar and the two pillars were given and fixed free by Messrs Walsh & Son of Cox Green Quarries.

2.5 Christ Church, Walmsley

Christ Church Walmsley, alternatively known as Walmsley Parish Church, has its roots in the Old Chapel described above. The church was built on the newly constructed Bolton to Blackburn Turnpike Road (now A666) in a position that was easier to access from the more populous surrounding districts. The site had been bought from Mr LeGendre Pierce Starkie and comprised a commanding position elevated above Eagley valley visible from many miles around. It seems to have included an ancient Saxon burial place, as various ancient relics were discovered when excavating the foundations, including a burial cist containing a skeleton, an urn and a flint knife possibly dating from the Bronze Age. The building of the new 'Christ Church', started in 1837 under the guidance of the architect Mr Edmund Sharpe when the foundations were laid. The architecture of the church offers an 18th century interpretation of an early 13th century style.

On October 3rd, 1839, the church was consecrated by the Lord Bishop of Chester. The cost was £3557 and it was consecrated free of debt. Subscribers to the Church Building Fund included: the Church Building Society £300, the Diocesan Society £300, Mr George Slater £250, Mr James Slater £250, Messrs James Chadwick and Brother £200, the Rev'd L Grisdale £100, Mr Thomas Wright £100, The Earl of Wilton £50, the Rev'd D. Hewitt £50, the Rev'd R Rothwell £30, the Rev'd Canon Slade £20 and a large number of subscriptions of 5 shillings. Some of the chief patrons and benefactors were members of the Slater family of Dunscar Bleachworks whose residence, The Holmes (later Galebrook Nursing Home), stands on the west side of the valley. Numerous members of the Slater family were Wardens of Walmsley between 1835 and 1921.

Many of the stones from the Walmsley Old Chapel were removed in 1837-39 and built into the new tower of Christ Church to create evidence of continuity. One lancet window was moved entirely and is now the second window on the right of the entrance. The 1552 bell from the Old Chapel was installed in the new church and used until 1883 when it was removed to the turret of the school. It is engraved *'Luke Ashton, Fecit Wigan 1742 Weight 67 lbs'*.

A newer bell, cast in 1882, 40 inches in diameter and supplied by J Taylor & Co, Bellfounders, Loughborough, is hung in a wooden frame in the west tower. On the waist are the words:

To the Honour and Glory of God
AD 1882
At the Age of Twenty and Three
Samuel Isherwood Gave Me
That to the Church I Might Call Thee.

The majestic tower of Christ Church, Walmsley in 2008.

Christ Church during a 'Weddings and Baptisms Open Day', June 1999.

Walmsley was created a separate Parish in 1844, but this did not fully come into effect until the departure of the Rev'd Canon James Slade in 1856.

Two beautifully designed silver chalices and a stem-paten were dedicated on Christmas Day, 1850, and a flagon and flat paten of exactly similar design and quality were dedicated on Christmas Day, 1868. They are inscribed Walmsley Church and the date, but the donors are not mentioned. The building was substantially enlarged in 1867 by the addition of a chancel, two transepts, an organ chamber and a clergy vestry. The organ was removed from the gallery, enlarged, and placed in the new organ chamber. The first extension to the churchyard was consecrated on May 20th, 1882. In 1888 more alterations were made to the church which included the installation of stained glass windows, a new font, and improvements to the baptistry. Further alterations, including re-pewing took place in 1889, the golden jubilee of the consecration. Beautiful mosaic pictures were erected on either side of the reredos, the choir stalls were altered, and the organ extended into the chancel between 1894 and 1912. Between 1913 and 1928 the organ was overhauled at a cost of £90, the church was practically re-roofed, electrically lit, a mains water supply installed, and the building re-decorated. The second extension to the churchyard was consecrated in 1937. October 3rd, 1939 marked 100 years since the church's consecration, and the Bishop of Manchester preached at the centenary service. There were plans for further alterations to celebrate the centenary but these had to be shelved because of the war.

In 1952 the Chapel of the Resurrection in the south transept - the Dimple Memorial - was dedicated following the closure of the Dimple Mission. There were also added, at this time, many new furnishings and ornaments including pulpit, choir stalls, and a new font from Bolton Parish Church. The chapel altar-piece, a 15th century Spanish triptych, was bought from a private owner in London by the late Canon Harry Nightingale, then the Vicar of Walmsley.

The south aisle and north aisle windows were designed by Sir E Burne-Jones and executed by William Morris. They are memorials to the Armisted family of Higher Dunscar. Another window is the memorial to the Rev'd Lowther Grisdale, who saw the church, the vicarage, and the school built. The east window depicts the principal events in the life of Christ. It is a memorial to the Slater family as are the mosaic pictures on the wall below. These are English mosaics with each tessera placed in a bed of mastic at a different angle to its neighbours so as to give a sparkling effect. The nave arcade pillars are stone monoliths (single columns), each 16 ft. high and quarried locally. The churchwardens' staves are made of oak from a ship in Nelson's navy, the Fourdroyant. The history of the oak is recorded on the ferrules and a list of churchwardens is engraved on the silver heads.

2.6 Eagley Schools

In the late 18th century Eagley was a hamlet on the edge of Little Bolton. There were a few houses, a bridge, an old mill, and the road linking Bolton with Blackburn. John Wesley crossed Eagley Bridge in 1781 and 1788 and described the pre-turnpike road from Bolton to Blackburn as *'miserable'*.

Eagley Day School's history began in 1794 with the building of Eagley Bridge School, started by public subscription. The much larger Eagley Mills School was built in School Street in 1851 and run by the mill owners. Strong links, albeit tenuous at times, existed from the late 18th century between Walmsley Church, the schools and the mills.

Eagley Sunday School began in 1785, in an unknown location, but independent of any local church or chapel. It catered for children coming from Eagley Bank and Astley Bridge on the south to Eagley, Dunscar and Toppings on the north. As well as providing religious and general education, it had a strong musical reputation and became widely known for giving choir concerts over many years. The Sunday School was linked with Christ Church, Walmsley from the mid-1800s although there were periods when it functioned independently.

The first entry in a minute book of February 13th, 1848 lists 85 girls and 75 boys on the register. As was then the case with other Sunday Schools, general as well as religious education was provided. When the new Eagley Day School opened in 1851, the same premises were used to house Sunday School scholars, with seven classes each for boys and girls respectively, under the superintendence of the Eagley Mills general manager with his under-manager acting as the Sunday School secretary. A harmonium was bought in 1852, to be used for hymn-singing, solo works and to accompany the choir. There was a Sunday School band from the 1850s. Concessions were made for scholars who also attended Walmsley Church regarding their arrival time at the Eagley Sunday School.

In the early 1860s the Rev'd Ralph C W Croft of Walmsley Parish Church offered to provide a Sunday evening service in the Eagley Sunday School for local residents. The management of Eagley Mills politely refused, but the cleric persisted and a letter of January, 12th 1867, explained that, as regular daytime services were being held in the school, they felt the morning and afternoon services were sufficient for the requirements of the village at the time, and again respectfully declined the cleric's offer. The day school headmaster, Mr J Mangnall, was also the Sunday School Superintendent from 5th October 1875 to 31st December, 1886. The Sunday School band was re-organised, banners were bought and the scholars took part in the Anglican School Centenary processions in Bolton on July 3rd, 1880.

Eagley Bridge School, built by public subscription in 1793.

Interior of Eagley Day School in 1901.

In May 1883 a pipe organ, funded by the Sunday School, was installed and Mr Joseph Greenhalgh, the harmoniumist, took over as organist. The instrument was dedicated and first used at a concert on May 26th, 1883 by a Mr Appleyard from Liverpool with a Miss Appleyard at the piano. The instrument was originally driven by a water wheel, then manually blown, and in 1950 fitted with an electrical blower.

Joseph Greenhalgh served as organist and choirmaster from the mid 1800's until 1923. He was succeeded by Tom Wright of Bromley Cross until 1948, then James Howarth until 1950, and Bill Knowles until closure in 1972.

There was always a great feeling of fellowship within the Sunday School which catered for all age groups. There were Primary Classes, Junior Classes, a Men's Class, a Ladies Class, football teams, a brass band, Glee Clubs, a choral society and a choir. Eagley Sunday School field day and festival re-emerged after the war in June 1919 with decorated lorries and carts, their young passengers bedecked with flower garlands as a *'Welcome Home'* for soldiers. There was also a *'Welcome Home'* for WWII servicemen in October 1946.

In 1929 a letter dated the 22nd October was sent from Mr F W Heap, Headmaster of Eagley Day School to the then Vicar of Walmsley which read: *'I am sending you an interesting book ---- it proves surely the right of the Church to the Sunday School here, and the position of the priest of the parish. It evidently became "independent" under the Gregs and Mr Walker my predecessors'.* The Greg family had a long association with Eagley Mills and schools. Arthur Greg was a manager of the day school and his wife Margaret Greg superintended the Sunday School infants and young ladies classes until she retired in 1919. George Walker, the longest serving Headmaster of Eagley Mills School (1887-1922) was also the superintendent of the Sunday School in this period.

From 1929 until the closure, Eagley Sunday School was more clearly identified as Anglican and under the care of the Vicar of Walmsley although the day-to-day affairs continued to be left in the hands of a superintendent and committee.

The Sunday School and day school in School Street is now a Grade 2 listed building and has recently been refurbished. The other premises have since been demolished and the area has been re-developed.

2.7 St Andrew's Church, Bromley Cross

In 1898 nearly all seats at Christ Church Walmsley were let (though rarely fully occupied by the holders). As it was sometimes impossible for newcomers to secure seating for the whole family to sit together, they either sought other places of worship or ceased to attend church altogether. Consideration of this and other problems, including the rise in population in the Toppings area, caused the Rev'd Chetwyn Atkinson, Vicar of Walmsley, to realize the need for a mission (or daughter) church at the opposite end of the parish to Christ Church for worship and other events. A local benefactor Mr H S Hoare offered one acre of land at his Toppings estate, locally known as the *'brick back'*, on which to build a new church. The vicar then purchased, for a very small sum (£40), an *'iron church'* from the parish of Haigh at Wigan.

The church when built was not to have rented seats, but free seating for all, and was to be self supporting from collections. The building at Haigh was dismantled and transported by horse drawn vehicle to Toppings and stored in a mill at Cox Green until the site at Toppings was ready.

The construction of the church was to be of timber and iron frame, set on a brick wall base and covered externally by corrugated sheeting. The interior walls to be lined with pine cladding, music to be provided by a harmonium sited on the left side of the chancel, and a font with an engraved base sited at the entrance.

Work commenced in April 1898 and on completion the building was dedicated on September 15th, 1898. Bishop Cramer-Roberts who was to have performed the Dedication Service was suddenly taken ill and the Vicar of Bolton, the Rev'd E Hoskyns took his place. It was named St Andrew's Mission Church but locally became nick-named '*the tin tabernacle*' or the '*the iron church*' because it was built of corrugated sheets. Several alterations were carried out to the building over the years. Refurbishments included the provision of a central aisle with two side aisles against each wall.

Later developments included the partitioning of the building at the back end to provide a meeting room for social functions. In 1974 a small pipe organ was installed by Mr J E Mason at the instigation of Mr Bill Knowles, the then organist and choirmaster. The church was beautifully furnished with rich carpeting, and chandelier lighting. Although originally meant to be temporary, it did in fact remain as a place of worship until 1988 when it was found to be structurally unsafe and had to be demolished. It was replaced by a new church, consecrated in 1994 by the Bishop of Manchester, which retains the name St Andrews and also houses the Eagley School War Memorial Board commemorating scholars who lost their lives in two World Wars

The old St Andrew's Church built 1898, demolished 1988.

Rev'd B H Lord with members of the choir outside the old church, c1935.

CHAPTER 3 UNITARIANS IN TURTON

3.1 Walmsley Unitarian Chapel

During the Commonwealth the puritan leanings of the ministers and the congregation at Walmsley Old Chapel were well established. Following the Restoration and after many difficulties in the penal times Presbyterians finally built their own chapel on a new site in 1713. It was a small, plain, low (14yds x 12yds), rectangular building, probably with a thatched roof. Today, the supporting walls of the chapel, up to half their present height, are original. The floor remained unflagged for many years and moveable forms with oaken backs were provided for seating. Early interments of the dead were within the chapel walls.

The chapel, established by trust deed, was erected on a parcel of land, 20yds x 18yds, leased by the trustees from Christopher Horrocks of Ash-holes in Turton, for the sum of £7. The land was subject to an annual rent of one penny payable on December 25th. The Horrocks family had control over who could be interred in the chapel or the surrounding land up to the mid 18th century.

The minister who encouraged the trustees to build the chapel was the Rev'd James Milne who lived with John Horrocks of Dunscar and married Horrocks' sister. The trustees were the yeomen: John Hampson, James Orrell, Moses Cocker, Evan Dewhurst, Ralph Orrell, James Kershaw senior, and Jeremiah Marsden.

In the original trust deed the chapel was to be used: *'as a meeting place and an assembly of a particular congregation of Protestants descending from the Church of England for the free exercise of their divine and religious worship therein weekly on the Christian Sabbaths or Lord's Days and on other days stated and occasionally, so as the ministers, preachers, teachers of the said congregation who for the time being shall officiate there, be able Protestant Ministers, preachers or teachers of the Gospel of the Presbyterian judgement and practice as to church discipline and government, and not of any other persuasion.'*

The chapel's trust deeds are remarkably liberal, as the only test required of the minister is that he shall preach according to the Holy Scriptures. They contain no creed or doctrine to which the minister is asked to subscribe his name. A published record gives over 500 people frequenting the chapel in 1715 even though it would only hold a fraction of this number. Interred within the chapel in the Year 1730 was James Milne who died at the age of 46 and served as minister of the congregation for 24 years.

More land around the chapel was gradually acquired from the Horrocks' family for expansion. A gallery with an outside staircase was added to the east end of the chapel in 1746 and the walls and roof raised. Two years later even more land was acquired from the same source for a burial ground and a minister's house.

A famous event is recorded in the chapel's history c1745 as follows. *'A gang of roughs known as the Church Party from Tonge Fold (the Tum Fowt Lambs) threatened to burn the Chapel down, but the sturdy worshippers resolved that no harm should come to it. The Presbyterians armed themselves with guns, pistols scythes and other weapons, and barricaded themselves inside the building. Having bored holes in the doors and removed panes of glass from the windows they waited for the attack well prepared to shoot any rash invaders. But when the besiegers discovered what a warm reception they would get, they considered that discretion was the better part of valour, and retired discomfited'.*

In the latter half of the 18th century, the change from Presbyterianism to Unitarianism took place. At Walmsley it occurred as a gradual process starting under the ministry of the Rev'd John Helme (1750-60). The Unitarian doctrine proved somewhat difficult for some of the congregation to accept and the transition was not smooth. There were attempts, when the Rev'd Thomas Davies became ill in the 1790s, to turn the chapel towards the Independent or Congregational tradition, but these failed. However a number of the congregation with Congregational sympathies, inspired by the Rev'd Richard Bowden of Darwen, left to found their own chapel, which developed into the present Egerton United Reformed Church.

Towards the end of the 18th century the chapel became popular, crowds gathered to attend services, and large sums of money were raised which enabled side galleries to be erected. This was during the ministry of the Rev'd John Taylor (1783-1789). He also built a new parsonage and had plans to build a boarding school but disputes with the congregation and choir caused his sudden resignation and departure.

The longest ministry at the chapel began in 1821 with the Rev'd William Probert and lasted up to his death, aged 80, in 1870. He was a Welshman, staunch Unitarian, scholar, and poet. On arrival at Walmsley, Probert had the job of removing a debt of £200. This he achieved, and later made improvements to the chapel, including the erection of a vestry, and the compilation of a library of nearly 200 books for the benefit of the congregation and the Sunday School. William Probert was a vigorous and practical preacher, his zeal in the propagation of Unitarian doctrines was only limited by his physical strength. He had developed something of a hard militant dogmatism and was contemptuous of what he described as that *'arrogant sect, the Church of England'*. He gave his best to

Walmsley Unitarian Chapel in 1888.

Blackburn Old Road, Dimple in 1953. This road provided access to the Chapel before the Bolton-Blackburn turnpike was built.

his people of education and learning in the days when these were hard to come by and his preaching reflected what he called '*the plain and practical truths of Christianity.*' Probert, a man of strong constitution, scorned the use of any transport and walked long distances to conduct services at Darwen, Blackburn, Bolton, Rivington, and Hindley. Writing in 1834 Probert described his flock: '*The congregation live in a wild hilly country and are much scattered. In winter time and in wet weather the roads are almost impassable; and besides, some of them have nearly four miles to walk to attend their place of worship'*. At a meeting to commemorate his years of service, he disclosed that in 42 years at Walmsley he had baptised about 940 children, and interred 800 persons in the grave yard. Probert wrote a succinct history on Unitarianism in Walmsley outlining the '*glorious principles of Non conformity*' The chapel came to be known locally as '*Probert's Chapel'*. He died on April 1st, 1870 after having preached the Sunday before with his usual vigour and ability, and was later buried in the chapel yard.

Major structural alterations and changes in furnishings were made in 1872. The roof was reinforced, the walls faced with pitch-faced stone and plastered on the inside. The centre area was re-pewed with open benches of varnished pitch-pine, with book boards and hat rails. The pulpit was moved and the communion table raised to a height approachable by two steps. A minister's vestry was erected at the north-west end and the outside stone steps to the gallery were removed. The chapel and vestry were fitted with hot water pipes. A new vestibule was erected at the chapel entrance with an inside gallery staircase of pitch-pine that also led to the organ console. An organ came from Bank Street Chapel in 1895. It was rebuilt in 1920 and a blower installed the following year. In 1952 a new blower was fitted, and the instrument was rebuilt by Mr J E Mason in 1976.

The first Sunday School connected with Walmsley Chapel was the Dimple School or Mission on Cox Green Road erected about 1797. In 1834 William Probert said that the average number taught was 100. He became Master of Dimple School between 1837 and 1850. The building was used for general education during the week, and used as a Sunday School by the Unitarians on Sundays. In 1850, the building was taken over by the Church of England, a move strongly opposed by the Unitarians. However, the Unitarians were not slow to make good their loss, and in 1851 they erected a new building near their chapel which became known as the '*Old School'*. In 1906 the building was extended by the addition of the '*New School'*. Classes and social events continue to be held in the premises.

For most of the 19th century the manse, alternatively known as the parsonage house or the chapel house, was sited on the Old Road. Access to the chapel was by a track at the side of the manse until the new Bolton to Blackburn Turnpike Road (A666) was built. Today, access is via a direct drive from Blackburn Road.

In the early 20th century the construction of the Delph Reservoir brought a threat to the chapel and the manse. In 1905 the Chapel Trustees petitioned the House of Commons regarding Bolton Corporation's plans to purchase the chapel, burial ground, manse and a small farm. As a result, in 1909, Bolton Corporation were only allowed to purchase a parcel of land together with the manse, at a cost of £1200. Part of this money was used to build a new manse at 578 Darwen Road.

Mr. John Bradshaw Gass JP, Chairman of the Chapel Trustees and a prominent local architect was buried at Walmsley Chapel. His grave and tomb-stone sited in the graveyard close to the main entrance.

The Sunday School at Walmsley Unitarian Chapel in 1986.

CHAPTER 4 CONGREGATIONALISTS IN TURTON

4.1 Egerton Congregational Chapel

The succession of ministers at Walmsley Old Chapel included the already mentioned Rev'd Michael Briscoe, who took charge c1652 This began the Independent cause in the area. During the persecutions after 1662 the congregation maintained its independence, sometimes by meeting in isolated lonely spots to pray and worship. Congregationalism in Egerton can claim a spiritual descent from Briscoe and the puritans of the days of the Commonwealth, who worshipped in and around Walmsley Old Chapel.

Walmsley Unitarian Chapel, built in 1713, was at first used by both Presbyterians and Independents for worship until a split occurred, resulting in the Independents leaving the chapel. They continued to worship in various places until eventually a room was hired at Eagley Mills in 1810 for around two years. Then encouraged by Richard Bowden, minister of Lower Chapel, Darwen (1799-1813), they moved to an old barn on Cox Green Road. At that time they attempted to move into the *'Old Village School'* on Cox Green Road but this was unsuccessful because the headmaster, a Unitarian, would not allow Bowden and his congregation to enter the premises. These continuing difficulties caused the Independents to want a chapel of their own and a plot of land was bought in Dewhurst's Great Meadow, Walmsley where the first Independent chapel was erected in 1814 by voluntary labour. The Rev'd Jonathan Wood was the first minister followed by the Rev'd Joseph Gill in 1818, who during a 28 years pastorate built up a strong congregation. He also established Independency at Belmont and his son was later a minister at Egerton. In 1873 arrangements were completed to build Egerton Congregational Church on Blackburn Road, now known as Egerton United Reformed Church, which was opened a year later.

Assistance at the services in Eagley Mills had been given by Joseph Sowden, minister at Dukes Alley Congregational Church, Bolton, one of the founders of the Lancashire Congregational Union and William Jones, minister at the new Congregational Church in Mawdsley Street, Bolton. Among the congregation who met in Eagley Mills were three men who left the Walmsley Unitarian Chapel: Isaac Orrell, Joseph Walsh and Jonathan Crooke and then became responsible for buying the plot of land on which the Independent Chapel was built.

An interesting incident was reported one week after the opening as follows: '*When the congregation had assembled and the service had proceeded a little way, a report was received that the gallery was giving way. And as is natural at such times, a rush was made to the outside, some by the door and others by the*

Egerton Congregational Chapel in 1888

Egerton United Reformed (Congregational) Church in 2005.

windows. After a time, order was obtained and the service was completed in the open air'.

The chapel made steady growth and progress with the addition of new members and financial support from a number of sources including the Lancashire Congregational Union. A new organ was played for the first time on Sunday 15th, October, 1837. When the national census was taken in 1851, churches and chapels were asked to make a census return, and the details for Egerton Chapel have been preserved. The chapel was described as '*Walmsley Independent Chapel, Village of Egerton, Lancashire, Independent or Congregationalist'*. There were 493 sittings in the chapel, of which 108 were always free, and the estimated attendances on the specified date, 30th, March 1851, for the general congregation and Sunday scholars were 240 morning, 274 afternoon, and 95 evening. There were 20 teachers at the chapel with reading and religious knowledge taught on Sundays and free instruction in writing and arithmetic available to Sunday School scholars on Tuesday evenings. It is also recorded that the less happy side of the minister's work included a resolution that illegitimate children must be baptised in private. Although the circumstances are very blurred there seems to have been a division of opinion in the chapel and, for a year or so, there was a second Independent Chapel in the village described as '*Egerton Vale Independent Chapel*' or '*Meeting House*'. The only surviving record of this breakaway chapel is a cash book dated March 1859. The two chapels united in 1860.

Among the members of the chapel recognised in 1860 was the father of a family which was to become prominent in Egerton. This was the Rev'd James Deakin, a Congregational Minister at Stand up to 1851, who had retired to Egerton and lived there up to his death in 1880. His son, Edward Carr Deakin founded Deakins' Bleachworks in Egerton about 1850. Edward Deakin, a seat holder at the Independent Chapel in 1852 and generous supporter in later life was also a contributor to the Egerton Vale Chapel.

During the 1860s, the pastorate was in the hands of the Rev'd Robert Leigh, and there are signs of relaxation among his flock. One new chapel member had been rescued from a life of drunkenness. He became convinced that he really was a sinner and of the deepest dye, and signed the Temperance Pledge. Another prospective member was diffident about exposing her spiritual feelings to others, and she, and others like her, were permitted to give their testimony by letter. Members guilty of immorality were excluded. A young woman was expelled: '*for gross licentiousness, followed by the birth of a child'*; and so was a man, deemed guilty of '*fornication with the person since become his wife*'.

The foundation stone of the present chapel on a new site was laid in July 1873 by Mr John Hayworth of Longworth Mills. It opened in August 1874, was Gothic in design and had seating for 650. The cost, £4659-9s-8d, was a large sum for the small village congregation, but because of the generosity of Mr Edward C Deakin and his sons this debt was soon cleared. The chapel had been built during the Rev'd James Clarke's pastorate and acquired the name '*Congregational Chapel*'. In 1892 it joined the Bolton Congregational Council, and in 1897 the Bolton Evangelical Free Church Council, both newly formed bodies. An official name change (for the registration of marriages) was made in 1901 to Egerton Congregational Church

Although not members, the Deakin family supported the church. Edward Deakin Senior and his wife were only received into membership of the church about 12 months before their deaths in 1899 and 1900 respectively. Their sons however, Edward and Henry, wielded great influence and support with Henry making a bequest of £2000 to the church in 1907. Two years later the church was placed in the trust of the Lancashire Congregational Union.

Children's work played a big part in church activities. In 1814 when the first chapel was opened, a schoolroom was also built. It had previously met in a weaving shop in a nearby cottage. Additional land was purchased in 1835 on which a new school was built capable of accommodating 400 scholars the original school premises becoming a vestry and chapel keeper's house. Although the number of scholars is not recorded, the school building became too small as numbers increased, so the school building was re-built and enlarged in 1902.

There was a vigorous social life at the end of the 19th century. The football and cricket teams were less popular than expected, and were disbanded after several years. The most popular activities were the Temperance Society for adults and the Band of Hope for the children. Other activities included Bible classes and discussion groups, a clothing club, a penny bank, and a sick and burial club. A holiday club began in 1911 and had a long and successful career.

Membership of the church flourished up to World War I, reaching a peak in 1914 of 148, of whom 115 were fairly regular communicants. The Golden Jubilee of the opening of the second chapel was celebrated in 1924, special visitors being Robert Hawarth, whose father had laid the foundation stone, and Samuel Gill, a descendent of the two ministers of that name. The Rev'd Henry Norman Hanstock, became Minister at Egerton in 1925, and was notable for his strong sense of social concern. He was a member of the Turton Urban District Council, and especially interested in education. He helped with the preparation of plans for Turton Secondary School which, after many delays, opened in 1952/53. Edward Deakin had resigned from the Advisory Committee; but in 1926 presented it with £5000. In 1927 an extension to the graveyard was dedicated, the surrounding wall being made of stones from farmhouses, closed on account of their proximity to the new Delph reservoir.

4.2 Edgworth Congregational Church

The first Congregational Church located near Four Lane Ends, Edgworth was initially known as the Edgworth Independent Chapel, built in 1822 and demolished in 1866. This was replaced with a new chapel founded in 1866 and demolished in 1964. The latter building was built partly on the site of the former chapel. A Sunday School building used up to the 1890s was sited close to the chapel on land which later became part of the graveyard. This was replaced with a red brick building founded in 1903 and well used up to closure in 1961. The building has had several uses since closure, including use as a Roman Catholic church, and is currently three private dwelling apartments.

The first report issued by the Lancashire Congregational Union dated January, 1808 contains the following passage relating to the introduction of Congregationalism into Edgworth and the first Pastor, John Winder:

'In April last, "the committee" resolved to pay a year's rent of a large room at Edgeworth Moor [sic], *a very benighted and populous part of the county; whither Mr Winder of Blackburn, has with steady zeal and unwearied patience, a long time kindly gone to preach in the face of many discouragements'.*

An *'Edgworth Church Book'* contains notes about Edgworth Congregationalism and gives some details about preachers who came to Brandwood Fold, before 1807. It is almost certain that an occasional preacher was one John Winder.

John Winder was born at Wyldes, Bury on September 13th, 1767, the only son of the Rev'd John Winder, curate of the Bury Old Road Parish Church. John Winder junior attended Bury Grammar School, became an apprentice printer, then moved into the fustian trade. He married Betty Philpott of Manchester in 1789, and had several children. About 1799 he went to reside at Rochdale where he worked as a bleacher. He then took up residence in Blackburn, became a school master, and identified himself with the Independent or Congregational cause.

He eventually settled as a pastor in Edgworth. His first preaching took place on Sunday evenings in a large upper room in premises known as *'Martin's Rooms'* at the entrance corner of Crown Point. In addition to his ministerial duties he taught a school in premises near the present White Horse public house then known as

Drawing of the 1822 Congregational Chapel, Edgworth.

Edgworth Congregational Church, built 1866, demolished c1961.

Bentley's Row, then at premises in Hob Lane which provided him with his main source of income.

Although the first congregation of Independents was formed in 1814, worship continued at Crown Point until 1822, when the first chapel was built. It was only 12yds square and became known as *'Owd Winders'*. The original deed was signed on the 18th, December, 1822 by 16 trustees and the chapel was opened in March 1823, the preacher being the Rev'd Wm. Roby of Manchester. The building accommodated about 400 people. On July 4th, 1830 Winder was preaching in the chapel when a severe storm occurred and the building was struck by lightning causing chaos among the members of the congregation.

In addition to Edgworth, Winder also started services at Broad Meadows, Entwistle and Whittlestonehead. He continued to labour at Edgworth until he retired in 1846 and died the next year on June 26th, 1847. His remains were laid in the centre of the old chapel and a tablet was erected to his memory by his sons which includes the following passage:

His remains lie in the body of this chapel. He was the first pastor of the congregation of Independents assembling in the neighbourhood, and founder of this place of worship, among whom he laboured as a dutiful minister of Christ upwards of 40 years, and went to his grave in peace.

During his ministry of around 40 years at Edgworth, Winder baptised 1220 children and adults. In the latter years of his life he rode about the district upon his favourite pony 'Bobby'. His name is still remembered with deep affection.

A new chapel was opened at Thomasson Fold on Good Friday April 19th, 1867. The building was in the early geometrical style of Gothic architecture, built of pitch-faced par points and gritstone dressings, with open timbered roofs, stained and varnished. It was planned to accommodate about 340 people on the ground floor and about 100 in the gallery at the west end. The stone for the windows, tower and spire came from a quarry near Isherwood Fold, Edgworth. Some local young men helped with the foundations, but the tower at the north-east corner was erected by a contractor. The west end, including the vestry and a house containing the warming apparatus, was built of stone taken from the old chapel with the date stone *'1822'* included. This stone has been preserved and is today in the care of a local resident.

The seats were open benches facing the platform pulpit. There were vestries for the ministers and the choir members, and an organ loft and choir stalls erected over these. The main entrances were at the east end, which were known as the principal front, one through the tower, the other through a porch with a neatly tiled corridor, separated from the chapel by a glass screen. A square tower surmounted by a neat octagonal spire stood at the north-east corner, 90ft high, a landmark which could be seen for many miles around.

The Rev'd Mr Dunn preached three times each Sunday throughout his ministry at Edgworth until his death on Sunday March 9th, 1884, after which he was interred in the chapel graveyard. A mural tablet was erected in the chapel and this has been carefully preserved by an Edgworth resident. It is inscribed:

'In Loving Memory of George Dunn as servant of Jesus Christ and for 50 years a preacher of His Gospel, striving by his example, his earnest teaching, and fervent prayer to win men to the Saviour. He was for 29 years Pastor of this Church and by his untiring efforts the Church and School were built. Born at Croft 23rd December 1818. Died at Edgworth 9th March 1884. 'I Have Kept The Faith.' This tablet is erected by his widow and children.'

An account in the Congregational Year Book for 1885, giving the Rev'd Dunn's activities in Edgworth says of him:

There is scarcely a house in and around Edgworth where Mr Dunn's voice has not been heard, either in preaching or in visitation of the sick. Formerly, when medical aid was not so easy of access as at present, the preacher prescribed medicine, and occasionally had to take the part of a policeman in quieting disturbances. Latterly he served the township by accepting the offices of overseer and member of the School Board. He took great interest in the Temperance Movement, being himself a practical teetotaller during the whole time of his residence in Edgworth.

Traditionally sermons were held on the second Sunday in May, when the outdoor procession walked through the village in the morning and the participants were plied with hot coffee and ice buns for sustenance before finishing at Miss Barlow's home, ('Greenthorne') to view the peacocks. For 'old times sake' the procession walked around Crown Point and Brandwood Fold. Visiting preachers were invited for the annual sermons services, notable the Rev'd J J L Clayton of Blackpool who attracted a large congregation. In those days, the church and gallery were packed full, and on many occasions extra forms were brought in which almost blocked the aisles. Ministers from other local Congregational churches officiated at some of the services after the departure of the Rev'd Clift. The Rev'd J W Evans combined Edgworth with the pastorate of Tonge Moor Congregational Church.

The Know Mill Printing Company at Entwistle closed completely in the 1950s and closure no doubt accelerated the decline in the local population and in chapel attendance. Both the church and the Sunday School buildings ceased to function in 1961 and the church was demolished c1967 but the graveyard remained. A house now stands on the land of the former church.

4.3 Whittlestone Head Congregational Chapel, Entwistle

Whittlestonehead, a hamlet in a bleak, upland moorland valley, is approached by a track opposite the Crown & Thistle Inn near Grimehills, on the old Roman Road between Edgworth and Darwen.

From about 1747 until 1851 a two-storey stone building in Whittlestonehead, owned by the Church of England, was used as a day school, a Sunday School, and a place of worship. Edgworth schoolmaster and Independent pastor, the Rev'd John Winder, who had been teaching and preaching around Entwistle from 1807 to 1846 began a school on Sundays at Whittlestonehead. Winder's successor at the Edgworth Independent Chapel, the Rev'd George Dunn, also preached at Whittlestonehead and was known to deliver a 45 minutes evening sermon after walking the three miles from Edgworth in all weathers and seasons. He was even held up at times by roughs on the old Roman Road.

Around the year 1851 the Anglicans transferred their school and religious activities to Grimehills School and the old stone building at Whittlestonehead became the property of the Congregationalists. The upper storey of the building was normally used for services, but at times like the annual sermons, which were regarded as a great event, both the upper and lower storeys were used and people even stood on the outside steps. For many years the preacher used an old box on four legs, located in one corner of the room. There was no ceiling and the roof was very low, causing the parson's head to frequently make contact with it during preaching. The window curtains were striking, being made-up of coloured tissue paper. Lighting was by a few fallow (brown or reddish) candles fixed in wire wall-mounted sconces around the room with one positioned close to the preacher. Not infrequently, persons were seen removing a candle from their pocket and using it to obtain enough light for hymn singing, after which it was extinguished and replaced in the pocket until the next hymn. The well known wealthy philanthropist James Barlow, of Higher Crow Trees, Entwistle, took a very active and somewhat paternal role in the place by superintending the school and sometimes conducting the services.

The hamlet became more heavily populated for a short period in the mid 19th century when the Bolton-Darwen railway line and the 2015 yards long Sough Tunnel were being built. Some 3000 workers and their families camped in huts

Whittlestonehead Congregational Chapel in a derelict state, 1960.

Whittlestonehead Chapel converted into a residential property: 2006.

and tents for up to three years. The railway authorised in 1845 and completed in 1848, cost five lives, and caused much trouble and unrest in the hamlet. Working conditions were tough for the navvies who were mostly ex-coal miners. The tunnel, driven through gritstone and shale, was cut in the light of flickering candles for most part. Many of the pastoral needs of the construction workers were satisfied and some education was provided by the pastors and members of the Whittlestonehead Chapel.

About the Year 1880 two cottages were purchased close to the old school building to be converted into a school-chapel. By 1885 the new school-chapel was built on approximately 260 square yards of land. An indenture of October 8th, 1884 includes information on the purchase of the two cottages. The buildings are described as *'an assigned cottage'* (a messuage or dwelling house with outbuildings and land), *'to be used for public worship according to the usages of Protestant Dissenters of the Congregational denomination commonly called Independents and being 'Phedo-Baptists'.* (The word 'phedo' used in the document is thought to have the same meaning as pseudo, inferring an imitation of the Baptists). The messuage was conveyed by a group of 17 local people to an elected body of trustees representing the congregation of members and communicants, known as *'The Society'*. The messuage was to be used regularly for assemblies to worship, for the instruction of children and adults, and for other religious and philanthropic purposes. Some of the seat holders paid pew-rents and gave or bequeathed monies to invest in government, real and leasehold securities. Part of the interest received from the securities was given to those seat holders who paid pew rents; the other part being used to cover insurance against fire, payments to workmen for maintenance and repairs to the buildings, and the upkeep and support of clergy and officers.

The trust deed only permitted those *'phedo-Baptist'* pastors who would hold, teach, preach and maintain the doctrines of Christian faith as set forth in the *'Agreed Schedule'*; a document which listed the strict doctrine and discipline of the society, similar to the Calvinists principles of belief. Any pastor found, or proved by reliable testimony, to be of immoral conduct, or who ceased to be of the *'phedo-Baptist'* denomination, or preached any other doctrines not in harmony with the *'Agreed Schedule'*, was to be removed from office if this was approved by the members. One of several strict provisos in the indenture was that the Society should have full power to manage all their internal and spiritual affairs including the admission, suspension and exclusion of members; and the election, suspension and dismissal of ministers, and other officers. The trust deed included a clause that if the Society should be dissolved or dispersed and not united again for six months, or if the approved form of worship be discontinued for two years or more, then the hereditaments must be directed to the Lancashire Independent College, or the

Lancashire Congregational Union, or to the charge of pastors of other *'phedo-Baptist'* churches.

Whittlestonehead Chapel, capable of seating 250 people, was 'worked' alongside Edgworth Chapel, and a Sunday afternoon service was conducted principally by lay preachers from Darwen and the surrounding district. The Sunday School had some 50 to 60 scholars at the end of the 1800s.

Although the Chapel was refurbished around 1927 the decrease in Whitlestonehead's population and the absence of electricity, gas and a mains water supply, together with a general decline in chapel-going, brought about its demise and eventual closure in 1938. After several years in a derelict state the building was converted into a private dwelling and named 'Chapel House'. The original stone plaque, now built into the wall of the house to the right of the doorway, reads: '*Whittlestonehead Congregational School-Chapel AD 1885*'. A marble memorial plaque listing the men killed in World War I with around 20 names is retained in the garden.

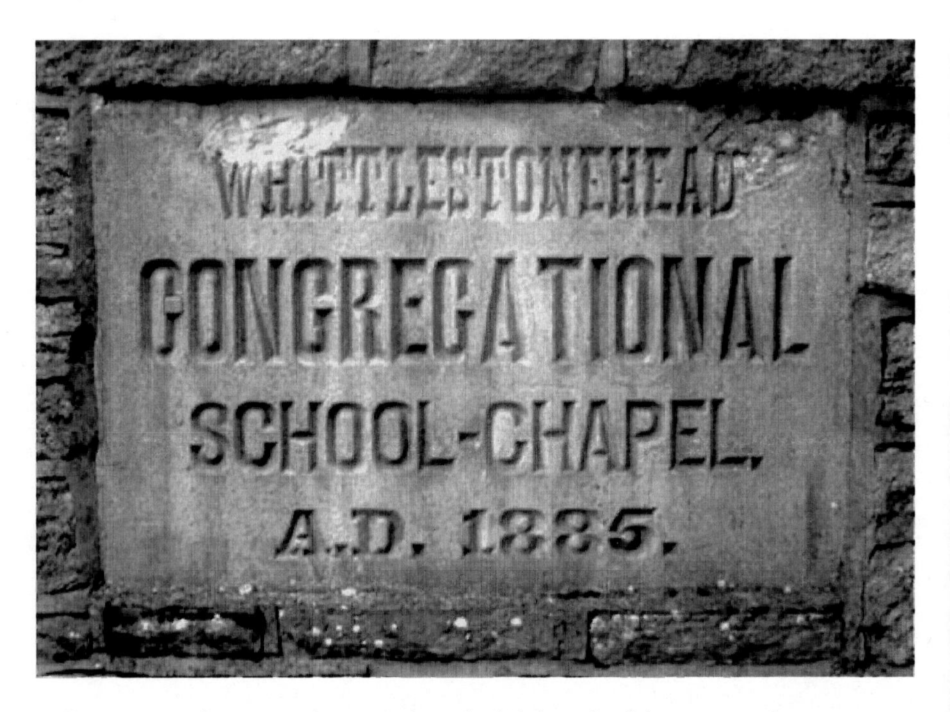

Commemorative stone plaque set into the brickwork of the converted property.

CHAPTER 5 QUAKERS IN TURTON

5.1 Edgworth Meeting House

The dissenting tradition in Bolton Parish continued after the Restoration and there were a number of registered dissenters' meeting houses in Turton, one being the house of Ann Entwistle, registered in 1689. During the course of the next century Quakers were active in Turton and a Meeting House at Thomasson Fold, Edgworth was founded in the late 18th Century.

An account of Quakerism in Edgworth describes that in 1760 a number of young men banded together and walked to the Quaker Meeting House at Crawshawbooth, some nine miles away. In 1762 the first Quaker Meeting (a religious service with silence and prayer) in Edgworth was held in William Lowe's barn at Isherwood Fold, followed in 1763 by a Meeting held in Thomas Thomasson's barn at Thomasson Fold. Thomasson was a farmer, quarry master and mill owner whose family had previously lived in the Edgworth area and were influential in parochial matters. Subsequent Edgworth Quaker Meetings were to be held in 1764 at Thomasson's house and at William Wood's home, Entwistle Hall, alternately, but when any specially large Meetings gathered they adjourned to one or other of the barns owned by Lowe or Thomasson.

On July 5th, 1766 there was a very large attendance at the burial of Sarah, wife of William Wood of Entwistle Hall, in the corner of a field in Edgworth. The field was purchased during the following year from Thomas Thomasson and fenced round to become a 16 yards by 14 yards Quaker burial ground. The next interment, Thomas Cooper of Edgworth, took place June 5th, 1770; followed by John Healey (or Houley) a well-to-do tenant of Turton Tower in 1776; followed by Alice, daughter of William Orrell of Heaton in 1777 and Hannah Taylor of Entwistle in 1781. A stone ledge ran round the inside of the burial ground about one foot from the bottom of the wall. Originally, the ledge was to afford seating, as in the early days of Quakerism worship under a roof was not allowed. Neither did they bury more than one person in a grave, or place stones over them.

In 1771 a stone Meeting House was built on the north-west side of the existing burial ground and paid for by the Lancashire Quarterly Meeting. It was used for the first Meeting on June 23rd, 1771 although the building work had not been completed. Teething troubles soon followed, and within the first five years the parlour had to be taken down and re-built.

The main founders of the Meeting House were Thomas Thomasson and his step-uncle and friend James Brandwood of Entwistle. Both were born into Anglican families and joined the Quaker religion at the same time in 1761. Brandwood had

The converted 1771 Quaker Meeting House at Thomasson Fold in 1908.

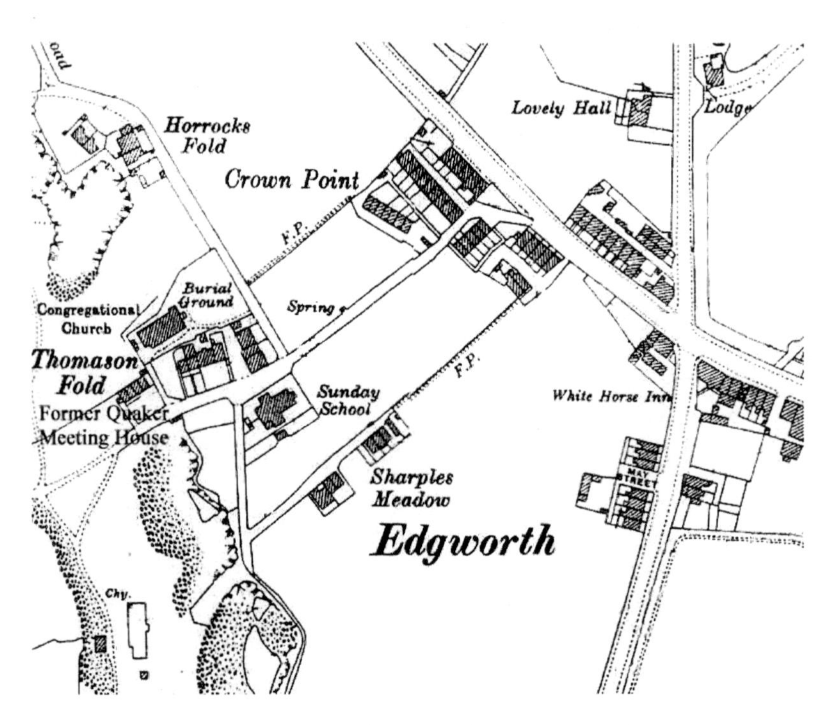

1929 OS map showing Thomasson Fold

The old Quaker Meeting House in 2006.

become impressed with Quakerism, seeing it as a simple and practical form of Christianity, that contrasted with the formality of words and rituals used in Anglican services. His conversion to Quakerism (his *'convincement'*) began in 1760. Other founders included John Ashworth of Windy Arbor, Edgworth; and William Thistlethwaite also of Edgworth; the two having married sisters of Thomas Thomasson.

Being used to holding Meetings in barns, the Edgworth Quakers favoured architecture in the vernacular style, as used in local farmsteads, and the design of the Edgworth Meeting House was typical of a Quaker Meeting House of that period. The building was essentially a flagged hall with benches on either side of a central aisle - one side for men; the other for women. At the front was an elevated stand for a lay minister; always a notable and respected member of the Quaker community. James Brandwood and Margaret, wife of Thomas Thomasson were both ministers. A stable with an upper room and an outside privy were erected at the same time as the Meeting House. Several structural changes to the building followed. An extra bay with an upper floor was added in 1788. In the year 1799 the original flagged floor was boarded and a cottage, now demolished, was built in the corner of the field adjacent to the burial ground.

The Meeting House was opened with some public display. They burnt their prayer and chant books, for which *'heresy'* James Brandwood, the Steward of Turton, was disinherited by his father. Links were maintained with the Meeting House at Crawshawbooth and with the Bolton Quakers at their house in Acresfield. In this way ideas were exchanged and support was more easily obtained when needed.

For several decades the Meeting House was well used until the strict disciplines and high moral principles of the Quaker movement, together with more population mobility and the influx of other people started to have an effect. As time passed, many of the old Quaker families moved, others lost their membership in the Society by *'marrying out'*. Young men and women were advised '*not to let their minds go out to such as were not of their Society*', a general rule that continued as late as 1863. In various other ways the cause languished. The Rev'd John Winder of Blackburn came upon the scene and started Congregationalism with such success that a chapel was later built in 1822 on an adjoining plot to the Meeting House.

A son of William Thistlethwaite fell in love with, and married, a young lady who had embraced Congregationalism, for which he was expelled from the Society, after due deliberation by the powers at Crawshawbooth, the ex-communication being couched in the usual ancient and quaint Quakerish phraseology. Another notable family name connected with Edgworth Quakers was that of Horrocks, formerly of Birches, who moved to Edgworth, leased a stone quarry, and started to manufacture millstones.

In 1837, after 66 years, the house ceased to be used and thereafter became known as *'The Old Meeting House'*. The Tipping Street Meeting House, opened in Bolton in 1820, had become more convenient for most families to attend. The lack of supervision by those involved and the increasing costs for repairs, precipitated the decision to finally close and sell the Meeting House, although the graveyard was retained and still remains the property of the Quakers. The main building was later extended and converted into four cottages in 1844.

CHAPTER 6 METHODISTS IN TURTON

6.1 Edgworth Methodist Church

There is some doubt about the date when Methodism began in Edgworth, but there is a record of a contribution of seven shillings and sixpence being sent from Edgworth to the *'Quarter Board'* of the Liverpool Circuit in 1771. This could well have been a donation from one or two families in Edgworth who claimed to be Methodists. When John Wesley travelled between Bolton and Darwen in 1788 he stopped to address workmen who were re-building Wayoh Bridge. He preached in Wayoh Lodge Farm Yard and at Holden Fold, now submerged by the waters of Wayoh Reservoir.

In 1793 preachers were brought to Edgworth village from Haslingden by a minister named Blackett and they *'missioned'* the people in the cottage in the Nursery, at Greenthorne and other places. Sunday School work in Edgworth started in cottages, one being at the Nursery. A little later a Sunday School was held at Tarkington's Farm on the south side of Entwistle Reservoir, and a regular bi-weekly service was held there on Sunday afternoons from 1802.

About two years later, the sale of a messuage, school house, cottage, and two closes of land in Edgworth took place. The deed records the sale of property from William Hutchinson Esq. and others, to Mr John Horrocks and others, and it was '*Inrolled in His Majesty's High Court of Chancery on the 24th day of December, in the Year of our Lord 1804*'. The following year there was a Methodist Sunday School in Hob Lane, led by Thomas Holt and maintained with the help of friends from Bolton, Haslingden and Darwen. Cottages near the Stone Mill at Top o'th' Holme, Turton Bottoms were also acquired for use; and in 1810, two *'places'* appeared on the Bolton Plan named *'Edgworth'* and *'Bottoms'*. The first sermons were held in 1808. As the Methodists did not have a building big enough for this occasion they used the Edgworth Independent Chapel's room at Crown Point but there were so many people present that the service was completed in the open.

For many years after, Edgworth Methodists held the only Sunday School in the village which, in those hard times, catered for children by teaching them to read their Bibles and write. Worship continued in scattered groups until a larger building known as Bridge Buildings (now the White Horse) at Four Lane Ends was acquired in 1813 for regular (and lively) services. The cellar of the building was used for hand-loom weaving and the ground floor was occupied by the owners, the Horrocks family, the leading members of the Sunday School in Edgworth. Steps outside the building led up to the first floor where religious services and the Sunday School were held. The attic above was also later used as a Sunday School after it was vacated by a block printing business that moved to Quarlton Vale.

Edgworth Methodist: 1828 Chapel and Sunday School, now apartments.

Edgworth Methodist: main entrance of the 1863 Chapel.

A large hole in the attic floor enabled scholars to hear the service in the room below. In 1816 the preacher at the charity sermons was the Rev'd Robert Spencer. There were 300 scholars in the Sunday School, 70 of whom were being taught to read and write.

On the Coronation of George IV, 300 scholars walked in procession to Chapeltown to join in the celebrations and although the Sunday School was large there were only 16 members of the society in 1818. The following year, one of the circuit ministers conducted a mission, the climax being a great 'Lovefeast' held at 'The Nursery', when it is claimed 1000 people attended and the membership increased from 16 to 100. By this time, Bridge Buildings was too small, and on special occasions like Charity Sermons, the Congregationalists loaned their chapel.

The first purpose-built Methodist premises were erected in 1828 to serve both as chapel and a Sunday School. 'Billy Dawson', probably the greatest Methodist orator of his time, preached the opening sermons. The building was used as a day school up to 1974 and a Sunday School until 1989 when it was converted into apartments. An important part of early Methodist activities was the *'Tea Meetings'*, recorded since 1837, that provided opportunities for social gatherings when there were few alternatives to entertainment in public houses. They were held on a variety of occasions including Shrove Tuesday, Turton Fair, Christmas Day and New Year's Day and began with singing and prayer.

The chapel always had a good reputation for hearty singing. In the days when services were held in Bridge Buildings the singing would almost certainly have been unaccompanied, and largely dependent upon a leader making a selection from a book of tunes provided by Wesley. By the end of the 19th century, the chapel had a choir, an organist and a deputy organist.

On August 17th, 1861 James Barlow Esq, at a meeting in his new mansion, offered £1000 towards the building of a new chapel. This, followed by other donations, resulting in a new chapel being built by 1863 on the opposite side of Bolton Road from the 1828 chapel. Opening services were held on July 24th, 1863. In 1896 an organ was installed and an electrically operated blower was added in 1924. An Edgworth Methodist Sunday School Plan, January to June, 1898 lists the names of the school officers and 28 teachers.

Golden Jubilee Year at the chapel was celebrated in 1913 with, among other things, a grand re-union meeting at which Sir Thomas Barlow, Bart, FRS, of London and other local folk took part. Records exist of the importance of a flower mission and an *'annual flower service'* during the first decades of the 20th century, Sunday School children were encouraged to bring flowers and bluebells to services for distribution afterwards, and bulbs were given to children to grow in their homes and later present the flowers to sick people in the workhouse and infirmary. At the 1911 Coronation Procession mothers were exhorted to make the occasion gay by letting their children carry baskets of flowers. A non-ordained layman, the popular Mr George Davies, is included in a list of ordained ministers who served at the Edgworth Chapel. It seems he was the only lay minister to serve there over all the previous years. As he ministered in 1918-19, his service at the chapel could well have been due to a shortage of ordained clergy at the end of World War I.

1928 was *'Centenary Year'* at the Sunday School with the celebrations presided over by Sir Thomas Barlow. Stained glass windows produced by Henry Holiday (1839-1927), one of the most talented stained glass artists of his time, were installed to enhance the interior of the chapel. In 1935 a Barlow Memorial Service was held in the chapel. The *'Chapel Centenary'* celebrations took place in October, 1963.

Interior of the 1863 chapel, the pews have since been removed.

6.2 Entwistle Methodist Chapel

A nonconformist chapel was built in 1872 on Crow Trees Lane, near Entwistle Hall, through a bequest of John Barlow. This building was once the centre of village life providing socials, concerts, early picture shows and religious functions. When first built it was called the Union Sunday School and used by people of different denominations but it later became more closely identified with Wesleyan Methodism. John Barlow died in 1870, aged 53, and was buried in ground earmarked for the graveyard. The chapel with its burial ground was included in the Bolton (Wesley) Circuit and had seating accommodation for 300. In its hey-day it provided a worship centre during a period of heavy employment in local industry especially in the Know Mill Print Works. The chapel closed in 1963 and its memorial plaque listing the men who served in the First World War was transferred to Edgworth Methodist Church.

Entwistle Methodist Chapel

Memorial tablet and explanatory plaque at Edgworth Methodist Church.

6.3 Birtenshaw Methodist Church

In the late 1700s, Wesleyans from Bromley Cross, Egerton and Eagley had to travel into Bolton to attend services at the Wesleyan Chapel at Ridgeway Gates. This was either on foot or horseback with little protection from the weather and no street lighting other than that provided by the moon on fine nights and at certain times of the month.

Continuing with the inspiration originally provided by John Wesley, Methodism in Bromley Cross grew and by the early 1800s local Wesleyans began to hold their own meetings. In Bromley Cross a portion of Birtenshaw Farm, located about half-a-mile from the present church, was allowed to be used for worship by the then tenant. A Preachers' Plan dated 1818 records that Birtenshaw and the Turton Workhouse off Goose Cote Lane were sharing the same preacher with the service times alternating so that he could travel between the two meetings and repeat his sermon.

By the year 1823 a new Sunday School building in Bromley Cross was being planned situated between the Volunteer Inn and the old guide post at the top of Hough Lane. This was to provide for the education of all religious denominations and it was agreed to build premises at the junction of Little Brow and Darwen Road. The plan matured into a small unpretentious brick building, later clothed in stonework, slightly set back from Darwen Road. The building still stands today as an old peoples' home. Visible over the doorway is an oval stone plaque which reads:

BIRTENSHAW SUNDAY SCHOOL
MDCCCXX111

From the 1820s to 1880s the building was referred to as *'Birtinshaw Sunday School'* (the spelling used in the mid-1800s to describe the village). The building later became known as *'Toppings School'* and later still as the *'Old School'*. It was built on land given by Messrs. G M and H J Hoare of Turton and almost the whole cost of the building was met by public subscription. Two of the appointed collectors were John and Robert Topping, who were influential men, land owners, and pioneers of Methodism. No trustees appear to have been appointed at the outset, the affairs of the school being managed by a joint body of annually elected subscribers and teachers. In the minutes of one of their monthly meetings is the first record of the founding of the Sunday School on November 5th, 1843. The meeting also resolved that: *'Robert Topping be appointed to officiate as Secretary until the next yearly meeting and George Kay be appointed Librarian'*. At the next annual meeting in 1844 the following officers were appointed to serve; as Superintendents, John Topping and Joseph Hamer; Secretary, Robert Topping;

Treasurer, William Sharples; Visitors, William Rothwell, George Haslam; Librarian, George Kay; Assistant Librarian; James Haslam; Committee Chairman, John Ashworth Junior.

By 1845 the first reference to a choir was made: *'that the singers' desk be removed further from the pulpit to make room for another seat of singers'*. A report of January 1st, 1846 states: *'The number of boys enrolled in this institution is 122, girls 140, total 262'*, which shows a healthy increase. The total number teachers was then 43 (29 male and 14 female). The report also gave an indication of a developing *'Wesleyan Atmosphere'* in the school. Wesleyan lay preachers, ministers, came from Bolton to take services and speak at tea parties. Up to 1845 all expenses seem to have been met by an annual subscription.

Extreme carefulness in money matters characterised all departments. Care-taking was a constant problem and school-keepers were short-lived. From the beginning, teachers had opened and closed the school as well as taken pulpit appointments. Plans were written quarterly for their guidance, and in 1847 a proposal was made: *'That the plans be printed'* but again, cost proved a barrier.

In 1851 the names of teachers and their classes started to appear in the Annual Meeting minutes. The names of 20 female teachers to 10 classes of girls and 11 male teachers to 9 classes of boys were recorded. James Cleworth was appointed Superintendent at this meeting to succeed John Topping. It was decided to purchase an harmonium in 1860 but it had not to cost more than 22 guineas (£23.10p). To instruct the young in the art of reading on the Sabbath was considered an obligation that was maintained until at least 1871. The library also played an important part in giving support to teaching and learning.

At a meeting in December 1873 a committee was elected to arrange to canvas the Circuit for funds for a new chapel at Birtenshaw. Trustees were appointed, a new building committee formed, and plans were prepared. Builders' estimates were sought and the lowest quote, from Townsons, was accepted. In 1874 the foundation stones were laid, and on June 25th,1875 the opening services were held after some vigorous fund-raising, by means of exhibitions, bazaars and sales of work, had made it all possible. A building extension was carried out in 1897 giving an extra 200 seats. In 1888 a new Sunday School was opened at the side of the chapel.

The 1900s saw an increase in social activities at Birtenshaw School with cricket, football, tennis, and physical culture classes running their cycles of popularity. Music also played a part in the development of the School. As far back as 1846 it was considered desirous to have a *'fiddle'* fitted up with screws and pinions, an idea that took a few years to be approved. In 1847 it was decided to buy an

The first Birtenshaw Sunday School, founded in 1823.

The above building after much refurbishment: 1987.

harmonium and pay a fee for Jesse Entwistle to learn how to play it. This instrument was sold in 1875 and a new one bought in 1876 which lasted for thirty years. A new hand-blown organ was installed in 1906, the benefactor being Edward Deakin of Hill Top, Belmont, with additional help given by John C Topping, grandson of a school stalwart. Levi Leyland occupied the organ seat for many years. A string band offered valuable service at tea parties, concerts and school anniversaries and the patients at Blair's Hospital were often entertained by the orchestra and choir.

When Moody and Sankey captured the country for hymn-singing their collection *'Sacred Songs and Solos'* was used for a time, but before the end of 1880, the new Wesleyan Sunday School Hymn Book came into regular use. A hired piano arrived in 1881 and an organ was sought in 1888 when the new Sunday School was nearing completion.

Although never elected School Superintendent, prominent community member John Ashworth Esq occupied the position of Chairman for over a quarter of a century. In 1855, the last Sunday in April was fixed for sermons which became the first of a long list of sermons anniversaries. John Topping was the first ex-school official to be invited to give the annual anniversary address. Since his day, many old scholars followed suit.

Temperance work started in 1862 when it was resolved: *'That we form a Band of Hope Society'*, but little progress was made until 1870 when John Ashworth took on the job of securing abstainers. Persistent endeavours during the following 30 years proved successful, resulting in a *'Band of Hope'* membership of some 600. A school report dated 1902 states: *'All the teachers and 90 per cent of the scholars are abstainers'*.

A Clothing Club existed in 1844 which served as a reminder of the *'Hungry Forties'*, and it again functioned in 1862 at the time of the *'Cotton Famine'*. Other groups included a Friendly Society, founded in 1864, a Burial Society, Social League, Guild of Help, Horticultural Society, Nursing Association, and Sunshine Flower Mission.

There were links with other Wesleyan chapels including Egerton Wesleyans and Cox Green Mission. On May 25th, 1895 members of the Birtenshaw Evangelical Association joined up with the members of the Cox Green Mission and had an outing by horse-drawn waggonette to Hawkshaw Lane. The Cox Green Mission was held in the mechanics' shop at Garnetts' Weaving Mill at Cox Green, Hardmans Lane. The mill was built in 1876 and closed in 1928. Mr J Garnett often attended the mission riding from his home on horseback.

In 1919 the School Council and Officers of Eagley Sunday School co-operated with Birtenshaw in a combined *'Welcome Home to Soldiers'* and it was decided to send 5 shillings (25p) to those soldiers who had not yet been discharged from the forces. A Tea Party and Concert for soldiers was held in both the Eagley School and the Birtenshaw School on Sept 20th, 1919.

In June 1922 Birtenshaw Trustees agreed that a memorial be erected for soldiers lost in the war. Funds were raised, and a stained glass window was installed in the chancel with a mosaic tablet below. The window, tablet and a communion table were unveiled at a special service after which *'The Last Post'* was sounded. Later a brass cross was placed on the holy table in memory of a soldier who gave his life in World War II. In 1964 a wooden plaque listing members of Egerton Wesleyan Chapel and School was transferred to Birtenshaw and erected on the chancel wall at the side of the memorial window.

Field days were for many years a strong feature at Birtenshaw, eagerly anticipated by younger scholars. The sports consisted of obstacle and flat races with tea, coffee, and buns consumed sitting on the grass. Sack races, three-legged races and egg and spoon races were enjoyed by scholars of all ages. Handfuls of sweets were thrown into the air for the younger scholars, this being one of the highlights of the day. Donkey rides, cricket matches and morris dancing were all enjoyed at the field days which were usually held in the field behind the church and school, before houses were built on it. Subsequently the field behind St Andrew's Church was used and the name changed to Birtenshaw Gala. In 1935 and 1936 train trips were arranged instead of field days

Around 1930 a decline in numbers attending Birtenshaw Sunday School was noticeable, in line with a national trend. In 1894 there had been 580 scholars, teachers and officers; by 1937 the number of scholars had dropped to 171. The decline caused financial difficulties due to falling income, which started to make the upkeep of a chapel and two schools difficult. Fund-raising efforts did not produce sufficient to continue with the three buildings.

On September 25th, 1932 there was a BBC broadcast from Birtenshaw to commemorate the union of the Methodist churches: Wesleyan, United and Primitive. The name 'church' rather than 'chapel' began to be used nationally after this date. The 150th anniversary of Methodism at Birtenshaw was celebrated in 1973 and the church is still active.

The Trustees decided to sell the old school in 1969 to avoid the escalating expense of upkeep and repairs. Its doors closed for the last time in December1970, marking the end of a glorious era of Wesleyan Methodism which spanned some 147 years in the old building.

Birtenshaw, based on a map of 1831, showing the location of Sunday Schools and Methodist chapel. The route of the old pre-turnpike Bolton-Blackburn highway is show by a broken line.

6.4 Egerton Methodist Church

The first Wesleyan Sunday School in Egerton was built in 1837 on Water Street. On Jan 31st, 1847 a teachers' meeting was held at Birtenshaw Chapel at which Mr J Chadwick, Superintendent of Egerton School, said, *'The Egerton School at present is in a low condition. Last Sunday we only had three teachers besides myself. Once we had 150 scholars, now we have only 60. Many scholars leave because we have no regular teachers. We would be glad of help'*. Robert Topping, a stalwart at Birtenshaw replied: *'Egerton is a branch school from Birtenshaw; we ought to assist and nurse it if at all possible'*. Four volunteers then offered themselves which helped Egerton for many years. Some Egerton School Superintendents were elected at meetings held at Birtenshaw, and ministers and workers at both chapels assisted each other, particularly in social and temperance work. The Methodists vacated their Water Street premises in December 1892 and they were sold to the Oddfellows and Foresters Friendly Societies. The societies agreed to pay half the cost of transfer. The premises were later demolished to make way for building the Egerton Swimming Baths.

On Feb 8th, 1890 the Chapel Trustees resolved to build a new stone school and chapel. This was to be between the Egerton Co-operative Stores on the north and Barry Row on the south. Subsequently a letter was received from Mr Ashworth of John Ashworth & Sons, agent for the land owners, which read:

To: Rev. T Brackenbury
24 Higher Bridge Street
Bolton

Rose Hill
Bromley Cross

Feb 26th 1890

Dear Sir,

Site For Proposed Wesleyan Chapel, Egerton

Your proposals have been laid before the exors. of the late E Ashworth. Considering that you wish to purchase the land for a place of Worship, they will accept 3/- per yard (square) the halves of adjoining streets being measured to you, and subject to such conditions of deed as their solicitors may find necessary. The plans of the building we should like to see.

Yours Truly,
John Ashworth & Sons.

Messrs Ashworth were requested to convey the land free of law charges. The contract for building was given to Henry Wardle & Co, Darwen who quoted the lowest tender. Building started but the firm went bankrupt before completion and the work was held up. The chapel was completed by the creditors in 1891 and included in the Bolton Bridge Street Circuit. There was one school hall, three other rooms and a chapel with pews for seating for 186 people.

The list of Chapel Trustees at the beginning of the 1892 minute book includes: J Rostron, A Brook, Sam C Brook, J Halliday, S Taylor, J Yates, A Entwistle, R Ward, W Greenhalgh, G W Walker, G Marsden, R Whittle, J Whittle, B S Thornton; fourteen in all. The chapel was registered as a place of worship on August 19th, 1892.

The possibility of organising a 10-day mission conducted by a Cliff College evangelist was considered by a meeting held on October 4th, 1909 when the Rev'd E C Harris occupied the Chair. The matter of Sunday evening preaching was discussed in October 1911 with a view towards improving attendance. A discussion about the distribution and recipients of the Lomax Charity took place during business at the November, 1912 meeting. It was reported at a meeting held on January 30th, 1913 that a park was in the course of formation and resolved that allowance be granted to remove soil adjoining the chapel free of charge.

Damage to the chapel rails by a horse and trap was discussed at a meeting held on October 18th, 1927. It was resolved that the rails be properly repaired at the expense of Mr John Oddie, farmer of Critchley Fold Farm, he being responsible for the damage. For many years, Thomas Middleton, a Chapel Trustee and engineer at the nearby Deakins Mill, 'patched-up' the heating boiler to keep it working and keep the place warm, but in the end the boiler failed and a replacement proved too costly.

Falling numbers of worshippers in the then small Egerton community and increasing maintenance costs, caused the chapel to close in 1963 after around 70 years of use. The structure is now used as residential apartments, but continues to proudly display its original date stone, 1891 in large numerals on the front facade.

The wedding of Dorothy and Leonard Scott at Egerton Methodist Church in 1945. Note all the ladies, including the organist, are wearing hats.

Location of the chapel and Sunday School in Egerton: 1908.

The converted Egerton Wesleyan Chapel building: 2005.

CHAPTER 7 BAPTISTS IN TURTON

7.1 Cornerstone Baptist Church, Bromley Cross

Cornerstone Baptist Church, Lords Stile Lane, Bromley Cross is an entirely new development, founded in 1977 in Harwood by Pastor Ron Stidham. He was part of a church planting team from the USA and his ministry was from the Baptist church with an emphasis that men must be *'born again'*.

When founded, the church was independent of the Baptist Union or any other local church and had a strong emphasis on evangelism. The congregation initially met in Walsh's Institute, Longsight in 1977, numbers grew, and as a result a new building had to be opened in Bromley Cross in 1984.

Cornerstone Baptist Church, Lords Stile Lane, Bromley Cross, opened 1984.

WEEKLY MEETINGS

SUNDAY
Morning Service and Sunday School 10:30 AM
Evening Service 6:00 PM
MONDAY
Young At Heart 2:00 PM
TUESDAY
Ladies Bible Study & Fellowship Meeting 10:15 AM
"Midweek" Church Bible Study & Prayer Meeting 7:30 PM
WEDNESDAY
Mothers & Toddlers 1:30 PM
THURSDAY
Cornerstone Brunch 12:00 PM
FRIDAY
JOY Club 6:30 PM

God Bless You at Christmas

Cornerstone Baptist Church

Where Are We?

CORNERSTONE
Baptist Church

Cornerstone Ambassador

Christmas '99 Issue

CHRISTMAS GREETINGS

Cornerstone
Baptist Church
Lord's Stile Lane,
Bromley Cross

The Christmas 1999 issue of Cornerstone Church news sheet.

CHAPTER 8 ROMAN CATHOLICS IN TURTON

8.1 St Aldhelm's Church, Edgworth

Prior to the Reformation, nearly everyone in north Turton attended the church in Chapeltown or possibly the Old Chapel at Walmesley. After the Reformation these, like all others, became Anglican and Roman Catholics worshipped elsewhere, often covertly, and sometimes having to travel great distances. In the penal times, a secret chapel was used in Turton Tower by the Catholics, but even this ceased to be available when the Orrell family sold the Tower in 1628 and thereafter there was no local place of worship.

Towards the end of the nineteenth century, the Bishop of Salford gave the spiritual charge of Turton to Father Steyaert, chaplain of Hollymount Orphanage in Tottington. He travelled to Turton to say Sunday mass in a room over a stable in Birches Brow. After his death, the practise continued until 1902 when Father Hampson became the first resident priest and St Aldhelm's Parish began life.

Shortly after Father Hampson's arrival he looked for more suitable premises and rented an old smithy in Turton Bottoms belonging to the Calico Printers Association. It was said that although this was an improvement on the previous premises, it would turn one's thoughts to the humble stable at Bethlehem!

Bridge House (100 Wellington Road) became vacant and it was decided to secure this as a presbytery and build a 'temporary' church behind. The ramshackle tin structure that resulted in 1909, served for 67 years! The structure may have been purchased from the Blackburn Road Congregationalists in Bolton, where such a building had been replaced by a handsome sandstone church that was nevertheless still referred to as *'The Iron Church'*. It is on record that the St Aldhelm's priest used to walk from Turton Bottoms to say mass at St Mary's Church, Palace Street, Bolton, then walk back to celebrate mass for his own people. Eventually the modern church of St. John the Evangelist, with adjoining Presbytery was opened at Bromley Cross in 1967.

There was much regret among the north Turton congregation regarding the lack of provision for their needs which led to the purchase, in February 1976, of the former Congregational church and Sunday School at Thomasson Fold, Edgworth for use as another St Aldhelm's. It was a handsome redbrick building that had been used as a factory for 12 years. Renovation back to a place of worship was entrusted to a parishioner, Mr A Ford, under the watchful eye of the parish priest. The sanctuary furnishings were made by a parishioner, Mr Bernard Ramsden, and the organ was donated by Eagley Mills Sunday School, redesigned and rebuilt by Mr J Eric Mason. The church was opened in 1976.

Due to the population growth in south Turton and the greater mobility of people with their own motor cars, St John the Evangelist Church at Bromley Cross gradually became the principal Roman Catholic church in Turton district. Both St Aldhelm's and St John's operated in parallel for several years before the eventual demise and closure in 1992 of the church in Edgworth.

8.2 St John's Church, Bromley Cross

The parish of St John the Evangelist in Bromley Cross was founded in 1960. At that time there was a rapid population growth in south Turton and a building was needed to cope with the increasing number of new families living in Higher Dunscar and the Hospital Road area.

Father Duggan, who served in Turton between 1960 and 1961 founded the parish at Bromley Cross by starting a new Mass Centre in a part of the parish acquired from Holy Infant's, Astley Bridge and St Columba's, Tonge Moor. This led to the building of the new modern church of 'St John the Evangelist'. The church and the adjoining presbytery were commissioned by Fr Duggan's successor Fr Hayes and opened on Sept 12th, 1967. The church was designed by John V Mather of Mather & Nutter, Manchester and built by a local firm.

Outside the main porch of the church, two bronze sculptures flank the main door depicting Our Lady and St John, the principal patrons of the Salford Diocese. They are in memory of Fr Duggan, who founded the parish and Fr Hayes, who built the church. Near the sanctuary is a fine carved statue of St John, in memory of Fr Hayes and in the Lady Chapel is a carved statue of Our Lady and the infant Jesus, in memory of the parish priest's parents.

Interior of St Aldhelm's RC Church at Thomasson Fold.

Undated picture thought to be of the interior of the old smithy, used as the Mass-Centre in St Aldhelm's parish, 1902-1909, with Fr Michael Pappalardo.

St Aldhelm's, behind Bridge House, erected as a temporary church in 1909 and used until 1976. It was sometime known as the 'Tin Church'.

ACKNOWLEDGEMENTS

Sincere thanks are due to the many people in Turton who have helped by sharing their knowledge, memories, documents, books, maps, old photographs and notes, all of which have made this publication possible.

The following individuals have been particular helpful:-
R Gwyn Atack, Pat & Alec Bagley, Anne & Hugh Bradley, Agnes Crook, Derrick Cooke, Jean Donnelly, The Rev'd Canon C Anthony Dorran, Malcolm Dowle, Joan Gilbert, Sandra Hall, Margaret Higson, Arnold Knowles, Bill Knowles, Maureen Mullarkey, Kenneth Ormrod, John Paton, Richard Pike, Pat & John Rea, Dorothy Scott, David Spencer, Jean Walsh, Clive Walsh, Bill Whitehead, Phil and Anne Windsor, George W Winward.

The staff at Bolton Library & Archives are to be thanked, as also is Jim Francis and committee members of Turton Local History Society.

The use of reports and photographs from the following newspapers is acknowledged - Bolton Evening News, Bolton Journal & Guardian, Bolton Chronicle, and Bolton Free Press. The front cover drawing is the work of Donald Dakeyne.

The literature on religion both nationally and in Lancashire is so large that it is difficult to include a comprehensive bibliography and references in the available space. Published histories are available for many of the churches. For a general history of religious development locally the reader is directed to standard sources such as The Victoria County History, Baines' History of Lancashire, Scholes' History of Bolton, and Lancashire Non Conformity by B Nightingale. Many of the important events and documents from the Civil War and Commonwealth period are described in the Proceedings of the Lancashire and Cheshire Record Society. Otherwise the works of local historians including those published by Turton Local History Society are also relevant.

Egerton Congregational Church Women's Guild in 1953.

Pupils at Christ Church School, Walmsley in 1980.